*With Love
and Squalor*

ALSO BY THOMAS BELLER

Seduction Theory

The Sleep-Over Artist

Personals (editor)

With Love and Squalor

14 Writers Respond to the Work of J. D. Salinger

Edited by

Kip Kotzen and Thomas Beller

Broadway Books

New York

Broadway Books titles may be purchased for business or promotional use or for special sales. For information, please write to: Special Markets Department, Random House, Inc., 1540 Broadway, New York, NY 10036.

PRINTED IN THE UNITED STATES OF AMERICA

BROADWAY BOOKS and its logo, a letter B bisected on the diagonal, are trademarks of Broadway Books, a division of Random House, Inc.

Visit our website at www.broadwaybooks.com

Library of Congress Cataloging-in-Publication Data
With love and squalor: 14 writers respond to the work of J.D. Salinger / edited by Kip Kotzen and Thomas Beller.—1st ed.
p. cm.
Includes bibliographical references (p. 193).
1. Salinger, J. D. (Jerome David), 1919– —Criticism and interpretation.
2. Salinger, J. D. (Jerome David), 1919– —Parodies, imitations, etc. I. Kotzen, Kip. II. Beller, Thomas.

PS3537.A426 Z975 2001
813'.54—dc21   2001035858

Designed by Lee Fukui

ISBN 0-7679-0799-X
10 9 8 7 6 5 4 3 2

In memory of Jerome Badanes

Contents

With Love
and Squalor

Introduction

There are a lot of things that most of us would rather not know about J. D. Salinger. What he eats or drinks. What he wears. What kind of father he is. Or any other of the various sordid details that have surfaced about his personal life in books by Ian Hamilton, Margaret Salinger, and Joyce Maynard. Personally, my interest was never in J. D. Salinger the myth. It was always in J. D. Salinger the writer.

The revelations made about Salinger's personal life in these recent books don't affect my reading of his work because finding out who he is can't change my own personal history of discovering Salinger. Reading Salinger for the first time made me excited not only about Salinger. It made me excited about reading. It has now been fifty years since *The Catcher in the Rye* was published and more than thirty-five years since he published his last book, *Raise High the Roof Beam, Carpenters*

1

and *Seymour—An Introduction*, but there is still intense interest in Salinger today.

While the recent coverage in books and magazines on Salinger has focused almost exclusively on his sustained seclusion, his romantic trysts, or his relationship with his children, what seems most interesting now is Salinger's profound influence on successive generations of writers. This includes a generation of young(ish) writers who are guiding our literature into the next century, most of whom were born at the time of or after Salinger withdrew from the literary world. But even though Salinger retreated, the writers in our collection were raised on Salinger in the same way that writers in the first half of the twentieth century were raised on Dickens and Twain. Salinger was a literary writer who was and has always been intensely popular.

Nowhere is the passion for Salinger greater than amongst writers. Writers have a different, very sensitive, sometimes quite introspective view of the world that Salinger captured in his work. For many writers, *The Catcher in the Rye* so defined first-person narrative that it limited the world to a binary option: a writer could embrace Salinger's loose, impressionistic, conversational, and above all untrustworthy and unreliable voice, or reject it for crisp, minimalist erudition. There is a cadence to Salinger's words, particularly to Holden's speech, that is incredibly distinctive. Salinger didn't invent this mode, but he defined it in his readers' minds. Salinger's stories, elliptical and yet precise examinations of relationships, of emotional toxicity, didn't conform to the previously established structure. His plots didn't necessarily make sense (at least not immediately), and the characters Salinger created didn't embrace traditional values. Salinger's narration and style were innovative, yet the issues that he examined were incredibly universal: conformity, loneliness, community, family, friendships, and relationships with the opposite sex.

One of the first impetuses toward the creation of *With Love and Squalor* was my discovery of a book entitled *Salinger* that was published in 1962 by Harper & Brothers. It was filled with very academic essays, most of which faulted Salinger for his feeble construction and his laissez-faire attitude toward language. The most readable one was by John Updike, but it struck me immediately that this book would be much better if it had been written in a less academic and more personal way. It was, however, fascinating to see how Salinger was viewed forty years ago. In the introduction Henry Grunwald wrote:

> The discussion can easily become obsessive and excessive. Perhaps we should all observe a moratorium on Salinger talk. But we won't, and John Wain has explained why not. Wain dislikes "Seymour," for all the usual reasons, and in fact suggests rather plaintively that Salinger brutally mistreats his readers in that story. But, he admits, "We won't leave. We stay, rooted to the spot . . . [We're] not in a position to go elsewhere. Because no one else is offering quite what Mr. Salinger is offering."

Grunwald, as well as Wain, articulates the close-to-chemical response readers have to Salinger's work, yet they both frame their praise with criticism. The debate on Salinger's merit has continued. There are those, such as Updike, Mary

McCarthy, and Joan Didion (who famously said that Salinger had a "tendency to flatter the essential triviality within each of his readers"), that think that Salinger's influence and import are overrated. Yet no matter how loudly they squawk, here we are fifty years later with reading Salinger still a seminal literary experience and *The Catcher in the Rye* being read by nearly every high school student in America.

The idea behind this book was not to make a paean to Salinger but to illicit honest feelings. My coeditor, Thomas Beller, and I approached various writers who we felt would have something interesting to say—either positive or negative—about J.D. Salinger, and gave them carte blanche. We chose to title the book *With Love and Squalor* because (aside from the direct nod to Salinger's own story) we found there is both deep affection and deep frustration with Salinger within the writers in our collection. It is not surprising that there seems to be a love-hate relationship with Salinger. The more poignant something is, the more intense the reaction it illicits. Some of the contributors have chosen to directly examine Salinger's work, and some have chosen to examine Salinger's effect on their own work. Others voiced their resentment, and others their unmitigated admiration. Many recalled the experience of reading Salinger for the first time, and have compared it to reading Salinger now.

In attempting to sum up this book for our publisher, Beller wrote, "We need people to aspire to, and we need to outgrow our role models. At some point you have to kill Daddy. Or love him. Or both." We did not choose the contributors for *With Love and Squalor* because we felt in any way that they were

Salinger clones. There is no such thing. But Salinger has permeated their work. I hope you will find the essays in this book a fascinating window into the sensibility of a generation of writers, all of whom are, in some way, Salinger's children.

Kip Kotzen

Good-bye, Holden Caulfield.
I Mean It. Go! Good-bye!

WALTER KIRN

It was a great book and I understood it. How great could it really be? I wondered. Mr. Durkee read whole chapters aloud, stirring his mustache and beard with puffs of air when he grew especially enthused. His impersonation of Holden Caulfield involved a compromise between his own voice—flat, midwestern, and modest in its vowels—and a lavish, nasal New England overdub that came in and out like a marginal radio signal. The effort of such complex enunciation dried his lips and forced him to keep licking them, which I found hard to watch. I gazed out the window at an old custodian weed-whacking tall grass around the flagpole.

My eighth-grade English teacher, Mr. Durkee, wore sandals with bumpy massage-nub soles and held the paperback inches from his glasses as he paced in front of the blackboard and performed, embarrassing us, as usual, with his commit-ment to raising our horizons above the ballfields and Lutheran steeples of eastern Minnesota. Between his readings, he spoke on themes and images. The word "nonconformist" was big, and so was "Christlike." I felt uncomfortable. He was trying to convert us, a couple of dozen unresponsive teens, to some sort of new philosophy or outlook that would set us at odds with our parents and our towns while granting us no clear ben-efits in return. *The Catcher in the Rye*, as he explained it, had helped to "radicalize" American culture and represented an artistic "watershed" in its portrayal of disillusioned youth.

Mr. Durkee so loved the book (the "text," he called it; an-other term that made me squirm and worry) that he insisted we read it twice—once at home, by ourselves, and a second time at school, together. His picture of our home lives was mistaken, though. Our houses were full of dogs and cats and siblings and noisy TVs and radios and telephones. There were lawns to mow and horse stalls to scrape clean and shirts to fold and even cows to milk. Flipping through *The Catcher in the Rye* and jot-ting our thoughts in the margins would not be possible for all but a few of us, and maybe none of us. Sure, our parents en-couraged homework—technically—but only when it involved digesting science facts or wrestling with numbers. Our home-work, if we were to be indulged in it, had to look like home-work, and lazing around with a slim red paperback about a high-school dropout just wouldn't cut it.

Instead we depended on Mr. Durkee to read the book for us, and then tell us what it meant. This was a better plan all around. For one thing, there were curse words in the book, and it eased my conscience quite a bit to let someone else be responsible for speaking them. There were penalties for such language, I'd been taught, and I was in enough trouble as it was. The usual sex sins, the usual petty thefts, the usual forbidden dreams and longings. Mr. Durkee, on the other hand, with his nicotine-stained skin and his slouch and his odd clothes, struck me as someone who'd shot his wad, salvationwise. A little potty talk couldn't hurt him further.

"Holden accepts nothing at face value," he told us after finishing one chapter. "He questions the value of basic institutions. He sees through social roles. The America of the 1950s was different from the nation of today—fearful about change, conventional, preferring stability over free expression."

Stability sounded pretty good to me. I was a raging conservative that year; I'd lived through about as much change as I could take. 1975, in the St. Croix River valley, was a plague year of divorces and teenage suicides and gas shortages and drug busts and mental breakdowns. The '60s had finally made it to the boonies and it felt as though my small town had been invaded by a swarm of psychedelic locusts. The Vietnam War was ending, but someone had spraypainted dripping, bloodred peace signs all over the library and the general store. The antique bandstand on the village green hosted a round-the-clock miniature Woodstock of blaring FM rock and stolen sixpacks and screaming matches with the constable. The last thing I wanted to hear about in school was the case for free expression and more chaos.

Not only didn't I welcome Mr. Durkee's ideas about Holden as a proto-hippie, I didn't believe them. This Holden character was a good kid; a privileged softy. Sure he drank and smoked a little and was given to moody, irritable funks, but he also fretted about his family and tried to do the right thing more often than not. Mostly, he just seemed bored and very tired. Funny, too, though I dared not laugh at him out of respect for Serious Literature. This was grave business, Holden's nonconformism, and when Mr. Durkee finally closed the book, he asked the class whether Holden was insane or if his "repressive era" was at fault—for being so hypocritical, so bland, so dull, so intolerant. The "era," we said, since we knew a test was coming.

To me, though, the era sounded, well, beautiful. The tidy parks with their flocks of fluffy ducks. The glamorous restaurants that served drinks to minors. The museums. The trains. The crime-free avenues. New York, as pictured on the evening news, was a hellhole of muggers and uncollected garbage, of sidewalks strewn with junkies' hypodermics, and to think that there had been this golden decade when teenagers could roam about at night there, checking in to hotels and blithely wandering—repressive? Hardly. It sounded like a blast.

. . .

MY FIRST COLLEGE roommate was a Long Island Quaker who spent the evenings playing acoustic guitar while I sat on my bunk bed and drank beer and tried to sing along. The songs were mournful, idealistic, sensitive. Neil Young. James Taylor. The hits from *Godspell*. When my roommate's fingers got tired, we played the radio—a New York folk rock station, mellow and uplifting—while discussing, oh I don't know, nuclear disarmament. We were terribly liberal, out to save the world, though secretly lonesome for our homes and families. The important big books we pretended to admire weren't sinking in as deeply as they should have been and I, for one, felt like a phony amid the ivy.

One night it came in over the radio, into our smoggy little Princeton dorm room with its paisley batiks and Jimmy Hendrix poster and towering stereo speakers and two-foot bong, that John Lennon, the Beatle, had been assassinated outside his apartment building near Central Park. My roommate collapsed. He genuinely grieved. I envied his responsiveness to tragedy and figured that it was due to his ability to picture the scene of the crime, which I found difficult, having never visited Manhattan.

All I knew of Central Park and its environs came from Salinger and Mr. Durkee. It seemed like such a cheerful place, full of strollers and charming eccentrics and young families. I decided to refresh my memory by opening *The Catcher in the Rye* for the first time since junior high. This was a big mistake. A Lennon mourner caught me in the act, grabbed the paperback away from me, and tossed it across the dining hall. Only later did I find out why. Lennon's killer, according to the news, had been fixated on the novel, and in its pages had discerned some sort of secret message authorizing his crime.

Now I was really intrigued. I'd gotten the book wrong again, it seemed. The first time around I'd missed its radical message about nonconformism and so on, and this time I'd missed its advocacy of violence toward multimillionaire rock musicians. I read it again, but I couldn't find the part that compelled Mark David Chapman to blaze away. This novel that had seemed to me once so breezy and straightforward—a couple of days in the life of a glum wisecracker who couldn't quite figure out where he was going and ached for all the people he'd left behind. But I had to admit the book had power. Wow! What power! To throw an entire generation into a social and philosophical uproar, as Mr. Durkee had taught, and then to whisper evilly in the ear of a grandiose music fan with a loaded pistol.

I knew by now that Salinger was a recluse, but I also happened to know that one of his children, a son, was somewhere on the campus, a Princeton student. I had someone point him out to me one day. He was tall and athletic and handsome. This baffled me. I expected an odder, less conventional creature. Someone with wrinkled slacks. So much for looking to life to help with books. Still, it was exciting to see the guy and have secondhand proof of his father's physicality.

My literature classes didn't help me deepen my understanding of the novel. The Princeton English Department, just then, was in a phase of high obscurity, and readable modern American authors such as Salinger weren't part of the syllabus. Desperate to take on the snobbery of my teachers, I came to regard the old hermit's books as classy young-adult fiction in a league with *Old Yeller*, *Black Beauty*, and *A Separate Peace*. The pleasure I took in Holden's voice (once I learned to distinguish it from Mr. Durkee's) was Exhibit A in the case against his greatness.

. . .

I PUBLISHED MY first book in my late twenties, a collection of stories on modest hometown subjects that featured several teenage narrators and reminded some reviewers of Salinger. This wasn't the wonderful compliment it seemed. Write about a white male under twenty in this country and you're sure to be compared to Salinger—never wholly favorably, even when the critic likes the book, and even when he makes it clear that he considers Salinger himself dated, minor, light, or overrated. Comparing young male writers to Salinger is code for saying they have a way to go before they become important, mature, profound.

The comparisons made no sense to me. My reactions to Holden Caulfield had always been personal, despite others' urgings to view him as an artifact of cultural, not actual, history. To me he was, above all else, an Easterner, and privileged in ways that I had never been. A gifted family, artistic, cosmopolitan. An expensive private education. Exposure to Broadway, to world-class museums. The learning, sophistication, and experience that Holden threw away in a few days would have lit up my small-town high school for a year.

The kid was sent to a madhouse, for heaven's sake, and madhouses were for rich folks. The farmers and Mormon kids I was writing about wouldn't have known who to go to for a reference to a respectable madhouse. What baloney.

But I picked up the book again, anyway. Just curious. It had been years and I'd forgotten most of it, which is always how it happens with novels I love. People tell me that the mark of a great book is the way it sticks with you, stays vivid over time, but I disagree. The best books fade into the scenery, dissolve into instant backdrop, return to dust. But that dust is never the same, it's changed forever. The book hangs on like a spore inside soil, and now and then it's suddenly reactivated by certain conditions of temperature and moisture.

The book had been reactivated in me every eight years or so. This was our third round. I fully expected that it would be our last. My intention was to erase whatever influence it might have had on my own beginner's fiction. Either that or determine that it had no influence; that my stories were as original as I'd hoped.

I sat on a porch in Montana, where I lived, far, far away from the scenes of Holden's delinquency, and sought to clear my head of Mr. Durkee, the dead John Lennon, and my Princeton professors. Too much static. I wanted a clear signal. Holden and I would meet out in the open, shake hands, and— I hoped—be finished with each other.

The edition was not the one I'd read before. Its cover was illustrated, not solid red, and featured a kid in a trench coat and hunting cap against a blurred background that looked like New York City. And though it showed Holden as Salinger described him and as most careful readers surely picture him, the image bewildered me. It was too fixed, too specific, too inert. Where was Mr. Durkee's young radical? Chapman's dark muse? The author's handsome son? Where was my own preferred vision of the character, the exhausted, cranky, preppy softy?

I read the book in one sitting, as usual, and forgot it even faster than in the past. I'd turn a page and look up from the porch, across the street at the neighbor's station wagon and his yard full of rusty tricycles and crabgrass, and the preceding page would vaporize. Good-bye slobby roommate. Good-bye old pederast. Good-bye ducks. Good-bye Central Park. Good-bye kid sister. At the end, Holden says how he misses everyone, a stroke that always comes as a surprise to me and seems both too broad and sloppy and too brilliant. I said good-bye to that, too, then shut my eyes. My conscious, definitive reading was

13

over, leaving me with . . . what? As a writer myself, it was time I pegged this book, assessed its technique, its style, its larger context. But nothing came. Just self-centered memories. Watching a school custodian mow grass. Singing Neil Young songs in a filthy dorm room. Hearing a radio bulletin: "Former Beatle . . ." Standing next to a mailbox in Montana, reading the first reviews of my own stories.

The best books vanish. I don't know where they go. One looks for them and only finds one's self. And then, under strange new circumstances, they're back. An editor phones (the one behind this volume) and tells me he's compiling a book on Salinger, and though I thought I was rid of that damned novel, here it is once more, open on my desk. How maddening. It's as if I'm being stalked. I'm sure that it's gone, that I'm free, but then I turn . . .

Mr. Durkee, was it the same for you?

The Peppy Girls of
Friendswood, Texas

RENÉ STEINKE

Before I could drive, I spent a lot of time lingering on the grounds of the church where my father was a minister, waiting for him to take me home. Next to the church, there was an ugly green building made of aluminum siding, a sort of gym with a narrow attic space upstairs furnished with cast-off couches and coffee tables. I was probably slouched on a mildewed cushion in that attic, in a kind of trance broken only slightly by the sound of car wheels in the gravel of the parking lot, when I picked up J.D. Salinger's *Nine Stories*.

It was one of a dozen yellowed paperbacks my dad had pulled for me from the bookshelves in his office. His spiky signature was inside the front flap, and the price marked on the cover (fifty cents) fit the book's glamorous origin in a different world, New York City in the fifties, a place I imagined as populated by men with very short hair who smoked and took a lot of trains, and stylish women who were a little sarcastic. Where we lived, in Friendswood, Texas, which managed to be both suburban enough to have cul-de-sacs and rural enough to have cow pastures, all the adults in their pool chairs seemed to be reading Jacqueline Susann, and the ones in their La-Z-Boys were reading fat books by James Michener beneath the fake Remington horses on the walls. My dad, who was proudly from the Northeast, gave me books that no one had ever heard of.

People who didn't know him well assumed he was puritanical, that he didn't drink, dance, curse, or smoke, and scolded people who did. He was more cerebral than fire and brimstone, but there weren't very many Lutherans in that part of Texas, so people didn't always get him. Men meeting my father would hide their beer behind their backs and say, "I'd better watch my language." One summer when he jumped up and down yelling at the call of an umpire at a Little League game, the picture made the front page of the newspaper, because ministers weren't supposed to do that. The televangelists and fundamentalists who ruled people's faiths down there were a sore spot—it annoyed him that anyone might think he was one of them.

I believed he felt misunderstood, and so did I. Being a minister's daughter was a little like being the child of a mayor of a very small town that assembles in their best clothes on Sundays. I knew everyone in the congregation, and they knew me, though they often knew me as a better, kinder girl than I really was.

My truer self hid up in the green building, where I read

with my feet propped on a coffee table that looked like it had once belonged to a living room set. Someone was always being misunderstood in Salinger's stories, and I liked that. Sometimes the misunderstood one turned heroic because he finally removed his poppy-colored mask, or shot himself in the head because there was nothing else to be done. The misunderstood character may have been lonely, but he nonetheless had an integrity that the other characters lacked, and he didn't try to explain himself or translate into simple language what couldn't be said. Though we didn't discuss it, I thought my father had given me that book for a reason.

The fact that the book was rare and arcane in Friendswood made my father worldly next to my English teacher, who I'm guessing only knew *The Catcher in the Rye* because she'd been required to teach it. She'd presented it to us dissected with reading comprehension questions, pinned each section down with "topics," and whatever life still beat in that book was slowly hacked away by the dull discussions. For me, *The Catcher in the Rye* had been so tainted by school, it might as well have been written by a different Salinger from the one who wrote *Nine Stories*.

Seeing the *Nine Stories* on my lap one day on the drive home from church, my father said, "I remember 'The Laughing Man.' What a great story. I think I'll always remember that mask."

Next to the sanctuary, my dad had a small office with gold-weave curtains, a wall of books, a shelf of golf trophies, a picture of forty young men with buzz cuts (his graduating class from the seminary), a black desk, and a couple of upholstered chairs. It seemed like an unlikely place for it to me, but people would often come to him there and tell him their troubles. I remember how odd their single cars would look, parked in front of the church in the otherwise empty parking lot. Most of the time I went to the green building to avoid seeing them come out of the office, their drawn, nervously laughing faces and tear-rubbed cheeks. Sometimes I would sit at the secretary's desk just outside (usually making a glue print of my palm), and beyond the door I would hear the vibrations of their voices.

There was Max, a young man with greasy dark hair that fell into his eyes, who was a drug addict. When he was out of a job again, my dad hired him as the church janitor, and I remember him nodding his head up and down as he mopped, as if agreeing with himself. There was Steven, a seven-year-old boy who liked to play in the rain and tell riddles he'd learned from the outsides of Dixie Cups. He had leukemia. There were pursed-lipped husbands and wives who came together or separately. There was the ruddy-faced jocular father of one of my classmates, who was having an affair with his secretary, and the short, plump mother of one of my brother's friends, who had passed out drunk in her car in the Safeway parking lot.

I found out these things because I overheard my parents talking or because people at church spoke about it in front of me. My father didn't discuss the meetings with me, but I could tell on the car ride home whether or not what he'd heard was weighing on him, because he'd smoke a cigarette quickly and his lips would move as he talked silently to himself.

Salinger's stories seemed to give form to the sadness beyond my father's office door. I was thirteen, moody and physically awkward, fond of what I thought of as serious talks. Though I couldn't have seen it then, Salinger's stories flattered me. They confirmed my suspicion that I was astute about human nature, that I was wise beyond my years because I loved this book no one had ever heard of. It seemed to me that I'd been prepared for Seymour Glass's suicide and could intuit the reasons why he'd shot himself, that epiphanic moments similar to the ones in the stories must have happened every week in people's confessions to my father. The Northeast settings resonated with my father's family history. And I was fascinated by the Jewish characters precisely because there weren't any Jews in Friendswood, and because I had learned some things about Hebrew and the Talmud in my dad's sermons.

But the stories also flattered me because so many were written in praise of girls, and I felt closer to girlhood than to womanhood then. Seymour Glass might not have been able to speak a true word to his wife, but he could hold a lively chat, full of poetry, with Sybil, the girl at the beach. In the house of the drunk, aging sorority sister, Ramona bravely invented her invisible friend, Jimmy Jimmereeno, so that she'd have at least one human to talk to. And Esmé was so charismatic, smart, and pretty, she had inspired an entire story. These were all melancholy girls like myself, as I saw it, and the fact that Salinger appreciated them made him a great writer (i.e., he liked girls like me). The only thing that bothered me about "For Esmé—with Love and Squalor" was that I couldn't imagine myself as both the soldier/writer and Esmé at the same time, and I wanted to be both.

In small-town Texas, the best girls were athletic, not thoughtful, with cute faces, not grave ones, and peppy cheerful manners, not distracted ones. My personality wasn't disposed to it anyway, but as I saw it, to be *peppy* would have denied too much that I knew and had seen. The peppy girl chirped "Hi!" to everyone, even those she didn't like, she walked with a bounce in her step, and in school raised her hand and answered only the most obvious questions. Peppiness had to be cultivated in Texas because the football team needed cheerleaders. *Peppiness* was akin to Holden Caulfield's idea of phoniness, and Salinger's stories helped to protect me from that ever-encroaching cult among girls.

It was obvious to me that the brittle, appearance-obsessed wife of Seymour Glass, the shallow, bigoted women who get drunk in "Uncle Wiggily in Connecticut," and the unfaithful wife in "Pretty Mouth and Green My Eyes," had once been peppy girls, and it had ultimately been their demise. Since at thirteen, I sometimes felt demoralized for not being peppy enough, I felt vindicated.

Salinger's deceptively straightforward sentences seemed to sing to me; the searching observations, not unlike the kind I had when I was bored or daydreaming, felt familiar. "It was a story that tended to sprawl all over the place, and yet it remained essentially portable. You could always take it home with you and reflect on it while sitting, say, in the out-going water in the bathtub." There were compact, memorable lines, part smart-aleck, part philosophical, that struck me as unpretentious and wise. "The most singular difference between happiness and joy is that happiness is a solid and joy a liquid." It was clearly an adult book, but it felt as if it had been written for me.

I've never been the type of person to carry around books as talismans or for show, but if I had been, I would have carried around *Nine Stories*. When I learned that Salinger hadn't written anything for a long time, it seemed to me only another manifestation of his extreme capacity for feeling. I saw him as a sort of mystic of words, with the narrow build and quirky manner of Seymour Glass. He may have been more symbol than man to me, but I still had a crush on him. His stories hung in my head like pop songs. Later, I would hear from my uncle that he remembered excited people lining up around the block, the way people now line up for concert tickets, waiting at the newsstand to buy the new *New Yorker* with the latest Salinger story printed inside.

But reading Salinger in Friendswood, Texas, in the 1970s seemed glamorously mandarin. I imagined that there must have been only a few of his books available in the world, that his stories were too strange for most people to appreciate, his genius only available to a few. There is something in Salinger's work conducive to creating snobs like I was. The characters we identify with are either too smart for their own good or too sensitive for their surroundings. There are clear lines between the shallow and the deep, and there isn't much water in between. People have to swim one way or the other. My snobbery didn't always last long enough to protect me from the peppy girls, but sometimes it did.

About a year after I read *Nine Stories,* the student minister at our church (also from the Northeast) gave me *Franny and Zooey,* saying, "This is my favorite book, and I think you are the kind of person who would appreciate it." *Exactly,* I thought to myself. When I read it, of course, I fancied myself as Franny, if only she'd been trapped in Friendswood, Texas. Franny is the perfect heroine for a minister's daughter because she makes religious questions not rote and pious, but alluring and dangerous. She even dares to bring them up on a date. She is also beautiful and fiercely smart, but not in the least bit peppy. "What do you think I'm doing in this crazy room—" she says to Zooey, "losing weight like mad, worrying Bessie and Les absolutely silly, upsetting the house, and everything. Don't you think I have sense enough to *worry* about my motives for saying the prayer?" I imagined what would happen if I fainted and began to say the Jesus prayer in our two-story Williamsburg on St. Cloud Drive, but the vision never quite held. It would have seemed Pentecostal.

I suspect that a lot of people first acquire Salinger's books as gifts, partially because they are flattering both to the giver and to the recipient. The young minister's gift also said that he was savvy, and willing to go along with Seymour's idea that the fat lady is "Christ Himself." For me *Franny and Zooey* is inextricably tied to that young minister, who I was fond of. It may be that one of the reasons people are so loyal to Salinger is that to betray him would be to betray the giver of the book as well.

When I left Friendswood, I saw that Salinger was in fact not as obscure as I'd been led to believe. And over the years, he became an abstraction, more dead than alive, an icon of silence, and a word, "Salingeresque."

I couldn't say why I didn't reread him for many years, except that there were so many other books I needed to read. But when I did finally read *Nine Stories* again, I was sadly disappointed. The strictness in Salinger's judgment, which had reassured me as a girl that peppy girls would get their due, now seemed to have a fanatic, unforgiving quality. It reminded me of a man I'd known who'd read so much literary theory that he deconstructed everything he saw until the whole world was fake. I suppose it's a workable worldview, if you can still remain cheerful about it, but in his case, it was paralyzing. It's hard to live in the adult world if you're that strict.

Though I fought my impatience, it was there. I saw through the cuteness ("The trouble with Picasso . . . was that he never listened to anybody—") and the charm ("See more glass"). I saw too much Glass everywhere, when before I had looked through the window of his prose as if it were magical air.

At the same time, something in me wanted to protect him. Was this impulse to defend him the same kind of attachment I might feel for a teacher I'd had in high school who seemed sage and witty at the time, but now, years later, when I see him on the street in his faded jeans and Indian-reservation belt, his pot-smoke-infused tweed jacket, seems sad and limited? Or was this the reverse of the snobbery I'd felt reading him as a girl? If loving Salinger's stories means that you are smart, perhaps even spiritually gifted, what does it mean when you don't find the same transcendence there?

I still admired Salinger's writing, the sharp dialogue, the eccentric observations, and I picked up on the humor, something I hadn't even noticed much before. (" 'That cat was a spy. It was a very clever German midget dressed up in a cheap fur coat.' ") "The Laughing Man," which made me think of Borges, still amazed me, and while "For Esmé" made me squirm, I loved the story no less. And I was still attached enough to this book that, in a regressive moment, I became outraged when I discovered that the singer Lisa Loeb had had the hubris to name her band after THE *Nine Stories*. That peppy girl had no right, I thought, to steal that title.

When the memoirs by Salinger's daughter and Joyce Maynard were published, it was clear from the reviews that other people felt a similar desire to protect Salinger. I was not one who believed that the women shouldn't have revealed Salinger as a not-so-loving father and seducer of young girls. In college, a poet whose work I cherished came to campus, gave a brilliant reading, and at the party afterward, with a few "poetic" words, drunkenly lunged to kiss me. I was mortified. But I'd learned then that the poet's gifts do not necessarily extend to his person. While hearing about Salinger's behavior only seemed like a sad repetition of something I'd seen or heard a hundred times before, the facts seemed amplified by their previous secrecy. The whole scandal made me feel old.

Nonetheless, there is something in Salinger that makes it difficult to separate the work from the image of the writer behind it, maybe because the work is full of so many writers, or thinkers who are would-be writers, that seem like stand-ins for the man himself. Knowing more about Salinger's life has made the stories seem less like mystic visions and more like accidental self-portraits. My reading habits may have been embarrassingly self-serving when I was a girl, but I would guess that most people reading Salinger identified closely with the appropriately sympathetic and confused characters. What had bothered me about "For Esmé"—wanting to be the writer of the story and its muse at the same time—is an old problem for women artists. But it seems to me that Salinger has a similar quandary. He wants to be Esmé, charming, full of youth and pluck, and he wants to be Soldier X, writing against despair, cynical and weary. The two sides argue with each other in that story, and the matter is never fully settled, which leaves the story, at the end, in a perfect imbalance.

It seems an even darker story knowing what I know now—that Salinger witnessed the worst of World War II, both in combat and in the concentration camp he helped to liberate (which makes X's nervous breakdown more harrowing); that he married a Nazi woman whom he'd previously arrested (X discovers a book owned by the German woman he's arrested, in which is inscribed "life is hell," and he replies beneath in writing that "hell is the suffering of being unable to love."); that he wooed Joyce Maynard through letters, not unlike the way Soldier X woos Esmé—this wooing suddenly seems much less innocent. This X is a man whose friendship with a thirteen-year-old girl helped him preserve his "faculties" after the war, only to return to his wife, a woman he apparently doesn't love, out of duty. The very act of the writing of the story seems desperately futile, since it's so unlikely that the essence of this thirteen-year-old girl (which he pines for) would still exist in the fully grown woman Esmé, who's about to be married herself.

Mary McCarthy complained about Salinger's narcissism back when he was first publishing: "And who are these wonder kids but Salinger himself, splitting and multiplying like the original amoeba?" She called his creation of the Glass family "a terrifying narcissus pool." Maybe it is, but plenty of artists have reworked fantasy mirrors of themselves into art (Colette, Cindy Sherman, Hemingway). The fantasy mirror can be part of a work's appeal. One of the reasons I found myself wanting to be Esmé or Franny is because I felt Salinger willing himself to be them too.

If Salinger is constructing the person he wants to be in the characters of these stories, or in the voice behind them—that of the mystic, the seer—then he is also revealing the less perfect man he is. Franny, at the end of the novel, may not be saved by her beauty and intelligence, or her prayers, and Soldier X is not finally saved by Esmé. I don't think Salinger is usually read this way, though. "Purity" is a word often used to describe Salinger's work, but there isn't much that's pure there.

If it was in clear delineations that I found solace as a young girl, what moves me now is the roughness. (Shapely, balanced narratives were not Salinger's strength.) The roughness might be the result of all the adult-life compromises he's omitted or torn out from the stories, or because Salinger is a frustrated poet. He might have been more like Rilke, the one Franny loves, if he hadn't been trapped in a fiction writer's mind. Rilke cries out to the angels, who don't really hear him, not unlike the way Soldier X writes to the thirteen-year-old Esmé, who long ago disappeared. Though what is lyrical in poetry can translate as naive and messy arrogance in prose, the attempt, in its very messiness, is poignant to me now.

What I wanted to protect in Salinger was my own thirteen-year-old self. I may no longer have to rail against the cult of peppiness, and I don't imagine anymore that every confession revealed in my father's office included an epiphany. But the sadness that was there still seeks a shape—and Salinger found it occasionally, even if the sadness was more misshapen than I'd first seen.

Salinger and Sobs

CHARLES D'AMBROSIO

In the days immediately after my brother killed himself I'd go into the backyard and lie on our picnic table and watch the November wind bend the branches of a tall fir tree across the street. Really hard gusts would shake loose a raucous band of black crows and send them wheeling into the sky. They'd caw and cackle and circle and resettle and rise again, crowing, I guess, a noisy mocking counterpart to the flock of strangers in funerary black who'd shown up to bury my brother. About a week after Danny'd put a gun to his head and pulled the trigger and a couple days after his lame orthodox funeral at our childhood church, I went for a walk along a street of patched potholes that runs around Lake Union (near where, a year or so into the future, a future I was sure had ended tragically the night Danny shot himself, my other brother Mike would pull a similar stunt, jumping off the Aurora Bridge and living to tell about it, thus revealing to me the comic, the vaudevillian underside of suicide), and saw a scavenging crow jabbing its beak into the breast of an injured robin. The robin had probably first been hit by a car. It was flipped on its back and badly maimed, but it wasn't carrion quite yet. One wing was pinned to its breast and the other flapped furiously in a useless struggle for flight and thus the bird, still fiercely instinctive, only managed to spin around in circles like the arrow you flick with your finger in a game of chance. The robin was fully alive, but it was caught in a futile hope, and I knew this, and the crow knew this, and while the crow taunted the bird, hopping down from its perch on a nearby fence, pecking at the robin, returning to his roost, waiting, dropping down and attacking again, I stood off to the side of the road and watched.

I'll tell you the ultimate outcome of this lopsided contest a little later, but for now I bring it up only because, some years ahead, fully inhabiting my aborted future, I often ask myself a koanlike question re. my brother that goes something like this: if I could intervene and change my own particular history would I alter past events in such a way that I'd bring Danny back to life? Would I return the single rimfire bullet to its quiet chamber in the gun and let the night of November 26, 19__, pass away in sleep and dreams or drink or television or whatever the anonymous bulk of history holds for most people? Would I uncurl the fingers from the grip, would I take away the pain, would I unwrite the note and slip the blank sheet back in the ream and return the ream to pulp and etc., would I exchange my own monstrous father for some kindly sap out of the sitcom tradition, would I do any of this, would I? And where would I be? Would I be there, in the room? Would my role be heroic? And where exactly would I begin digging into the past, making corrections, amending it? How far back do I have to go to undo the whole dark kit and caboodle? I mean from where I sit now I can imagine a vast sordid history finally reaching its penultimate unraveled state in the Garden, under the shade of the tree of knowledge, begging the question of whether or not I'd halt the innocent hand, leaving the apple alone, unbitten.

I'm a little wary of prelapsarian schemes in much the same way I'm leery of conspiracy theories, both of which only seem to describe the limitations, like Hamlet's nutshell, of the holder's mind. You don't really want to crash down the whole universe just to satisfy your situational unease or your incapacity to see the whole picture, do you? You don't want a life based on your failure to understand life, right? If I were able to undo Danny's death would that mean, too, that Mike's suicide attempt would never occur, or would it simply mean that he'd find an alternate, more surefire lethality than leaping over the rail of Seattle's most famous suicide spot, a spot that's worked just hunky-dory for hundreds of others? Or would my remaining brother drown or die of internal injuries instead of, as it turned out, smacking the water, breaking his pelvis, destroying his bladder, dislocating his shoulder and yet, that screwed up (plus I forgot to mention his chronic schizophrenia), still having the presence of mind to kick off his boots, swim for shore, pull a quarter out of his pants, and call an ambulance for himself, easy as a man catching a cab? Would that little miracle not happen in this revamped history of mine? Would I just be trading one brother for another? Would I even be writing this, or would a lovely silence reign over my uneventful life, leaving me free to consider other, happier fortunes?

. . .

I'D NEVER READ J.D. Salinger or John Knowles, both staples of the high-school curriculum, because somehow out of the always ripening ambient culture I'd picked up a whiff of the East Coast, of the uppercrust and hoity-toity and, ipso facto, at least for me, a kind of irrelevance, irrelevance tinged with a defensive countersnobbery that's so characteristic of the West. I couldn't identify with the prep-school scene. I thought it was socially atavistic, some stupid idea invented in England. So instead of the boarding-school experiences of Salinger or Knowles I read Joyce's *Portrait of the Artist as a Young Man* strictly for its creepy Jesuit milieu and the way Stephen Dedalus used difference and snobbery to escape. The reading of *Portrait* was itself a Dedalean act of snobbery on my part, a pose I hoped would piss off the jocks at my Jesuit boys' school. Why? Because I *was* a jock, but had recently quit all sports in order to take up managing my misery full-time. At that age, at sixteen, seventeen, I read fiction because I needed advice on how to live, and I needed it to be totally free of judgment. I wanted to see how other people did life. I had exiled myself from the kind of order found on the athletic field, and the alternatives that presented themselves most obviously at my school were to become a dope fiend or a scholar. I tried both and bookishness stuck. By reading I hoped to get as far as I could from Catholic homiletics, and quickly discovered that the best place for moral-free advice was really good fiction. Immediately I saw that stories looked squarely and bravely at lives without criticizing or condemning them. Admittedly, wanting practical advice is a pretty primitive idea of what a book should do, but that's the sort of literary sense I had, treating novels and stories like the self-help manuals that cycle through the decades, reinventing relevance. I didn't know any better, and probably still don't. Anyway, I came late to *The Catcher in the Rye*, as an adult, and thought I'd be somewhat cold to its charms.

I wasn't. Right from the beginning my reading of Salinger's work was lopsided, eccentric, obsessed with the reclusive writer's legendary silence and the theme of suicide that seems to stitch a quilt out of the extant work. As is always, perhaps inevitably, the case, the unbalanced weight my own life brought to the material gave the work this off-center, wobbly orbit, and even now I can't seem to read the stuff any differently. It's all about Suicide and Silence. Suicide is first mentioned when Holden, standing on a hill above the football field, says the game with Saxon Hall "was the last game of the year, and you were supposed to commit suicide or something if old Pencey didn't win." Other direct mentions of suicide or thinly veiled threats run through the story. The very word has a casual suggestive presence in Holden's vocabulary. He volunteers to ride on top of the next atomic bomb. And then there's the story he tells of James Castle, the boy who leaps from the window, killing himself, while wearing a black turtleneck he'd borrowed from Holden. It's now generally a given in the literature of suicidology that every attempt is ambivalent, that some degree of chance is worked into each plan, a savior chosen, an opportunity for rescue extended, a tortured hope hidden near the heart of the suicide's rapidly constricting universe. For instance, suicides tend to move *toward* society—and possible intervention—the closer they come to making and carrying out concrete plans. And of course *The Catcher in the Rye* takes its title from precisely this sort of ambivalence, and the story itself, in some ways an extended riff on saving and being saved, is otherwise full of specific strategies for rescue—with Holden nervously alternating point of view, vacillating between rescuer and rescued.

The passage below gives the book its name and is obviously as much about Holden's hope for himself as it is about the fantasy of saving others:

> I keep picturing all these little kids playing some game in this big field of rye and all. Thousands of little kids, and nobody's around—nobody big, I mean—except me. And I'm standing on the edge of some crazy cliff. What I have to do, I have to catch everybody if they start to go over the cliff—I mean if they're running and they don't look where they're going I have to come out from somewhere and catch them. That's all I'd do all day. I'd just be the catcher in the rye . . .

I generally don't read biographical gossip about writers, and don't know a thing, not one scrap, about Salinger's life (other than the silence), but the theme of suicide feels authentic to me, and so does his recurrent big family thing, two elements I share with—who? Salinger, or his various narrators, or both? I don't know. Like the Glasses (let's say), we too had seven kids, and one thing that seems to happen in large families more often than in small is that nicknames flourish, partly because there's always some little kid around who can't pronounce the real names of his older siblings. Little kids forming their first syllables corrupt those names, and the corruptions stick because they're cute or funny or whatever. Salinger's Glass family seems to be all nicknames except for Seymour. As the oldest child, I too was somewhat exempt—more namer than named—but a good example of the process from our family would be my sister Patricia, who quickly migrated from Tricia to Trish and then skipped sideways to Didya before finally arriving at Did. And Did's sisters were Mugs, Gith, and Bean, and Did called my brother Danny Mr. Sobs, or plain Sobs, because when they played house he was always the baby. These goofed-up, singsong names recall Franny, Zooey, Boo Boo, etc. And too, in large families, children form their own fairly populous society, separate from the parents, and the nicknames become a kind of argot, a secret language, whereas in small families, I imagine, there's more of an emphasis on vertical and direct contact with the adults. Anyway, Salinger's use of nicknames, the proliferation of them, and the fact that the oldest, Seymour, doesn't have one, has always been for me an important detail in understanding the work.

In Salinger's work, there is an ongoing failure of the various narrators that occupy center stage, a failure to find a separate and distinct identity outside the corporate idea of family. Holden is a little bit D.B. and Allie and Phoebe, and Buddy is Seymour and Zooey, etc., etc. People from big families tend to have this intense group identity. I don't know why, even though, for instance, I fall easily into the first-person plural when asked about my past. My gut instinct, looking back, is to

use "we." Is it size alone that accounts for the blurring of identity in a big family? The fact that you grow up crowded into
the same bathroom, brushing your teeth in front of a mirror
that has three or four other foamy white grins reflecting back
at you, is that it? Or the way you end up wearing some other
kid's clothes, or finding a favorite outfit, years after you last
wore it, in your brother's drawer, as if he were just another,
later edition of you—is that it? Possibly. Privacy, too, is a problem. You rarely get time alone. And with so many competing
parties, a constantly negotiated peace accord is necessary if you
hope to get along; and for the simplest things, for using a car
on Friday night or choosing a channel on the television, you
end up working closely, and in concert, with the other kids. In
our house, taking this closeness a step further, we institution-
alized the buddy system, a permanent arrangement in which
every older kid was assigned a younger, and you were strictly
accountable for that child's safety at crosswalks as well as his
mischief in the aisles of supermarkets and his happiness during
the long wait to buy new play-shoes at Penny's. As the oldest,
my assigned buddy was my brother Danny, the youngest and
rowdiest.

For Salinger's narrators, there's never sufficient separation
from the family, at least that sense of family defined horizon-
tally by siblings. Holden really only loves D.B., his dead
brother Allie, and his sister Phoebe, mistrusting everyone else.
Nobody outside the circle of family seems to make any sense
to him, or at least they aren't given the same ample room for
oddity he grants his brothers and sisters. Other people simply
aren't real to Holden, not in the solid, reassuring way family is.
My point here, in discussing identity and family, isn't to draw

near a psychological reading of the work. In fact, it seems to me that the decade of the fifties, which saw the first flush of a mass psychological processing of life, right away meets in Holden Caulfield its staunchest resistance. (In *Seymour—An Introduction*, Salinger writes of the psychiatric profession: "They're a peerage of tin ears. With such faulty equipment, with those ears, how can anyone possibly trace the pain, by sound and quality alone, back to its source? With such wretched hearing equipment, the best, I think, that can be detected, and perhaps verified, is a few stray, thin overtones—hardly even counterpoint—coming from a troubled childhood or a disordered libido.") There doesn't *seem* to be anything really wrong with Holden, and yet everything is messed up. The conceit of the novel is that Holden's telling the story from inside an institution, and you can imagine, you can *hear* in the loud nervous prose, that he's making a direct appeal to the reader, going over the heads of doctors and nurses and various experts who don't get it.

The subject of big families might seem fringy but it brings me to the organizing idea of authenticity. It's a central question in all the work. What is real? What is trustworthy? Holden, of course, is famously on guard against phonies, watchful for insincere people or hypocrites, anyone giving a false impression, the pretentious, impostors and perverts. In "Bananafish" the trite phone conversation—the false narrative—between the wife and her mother is brutally wrong about Seymour. It's untrue, it says nothing real or accurate about the world. And Buddy Glass, the narrator in *Seymour—An Introduction*, says, "I can usually tell whether a poet or prose writer is drawing from the first-, second-, or tenth-hand experience or is foisting off on us what he'd like to think is pure invention." It's not so much the content of this statement but the very issue of authenticity that piques my interest. The ability to detect authenticity is a critical faculty, something all of us develop, more or less. You can fail on either side, you can be gullible, easily duped, or you can be too skeptical, believing nothing. And with Holden, for example, it's quite clear that something else, a voracious doubt, is driving him to question even the simplest interactions with people. *Nothing* is authentic for Holden, and his problem is not so much a superficial sorting of the true from the false—he can't figure out how we come to know anything at all. That's the noise, the frightening disturbance in the story, and it will only stop when Holden finds the authentic thing, the real (what?), or when he's too exhausted to continue.

What can Holden rely on, what does he trust, what's real for him? Holden's response to life is like a body in shock, to withdraw into the core of identity, in his case the family, in order to keep the self functioning and alive. There's a love and warmth and security to the way Salinger writes about family, a kind of bulwarked intimacy most readers respond to, that sits in contrast to the false, unfriendly, wolfish world huffing and puffing right outside the door. What I feel reading Salinger is an emotional power that comes from the writer's ingrained *assumption* of the value and integrity of family, in particular the idea of family defined by siblings. Family is worthy of trust. The siblings in Salinger are fiercely loyal and extremely close to one another. So there's that clear separation of family from everyone else, but something in-between is missing, some understanding—for the writer, and for Holden. Holden can't negotiate the boundaries between himself and others—Antolini's touch freaks him out—and can only imagine returning to his family as a refuge. But it's my suspicion that that refuge isn't really a haven the way Holden imagines it—nor is it safe for Salinger, who seems to defang his work by taking the parents out of almost every story. You wonder, where are the adults in this world that's populated almost solely by precocious children?

This is guesswork, this is supposition: the real stress in Holden's life comes from having no safe place, with his family offering him the least security of all. This remains unstated *on purpose*. In the injunctive first paragraph of *The Catcher in the Rye*, Holden says his parents would have "about two hemorrhages apiece" if he "told anything pretty personal about them. They're quite touchy about anything like that, especially my father. They're *nice* and all—I'm not saying that—but they're also touchy as hell." It's that "touch," rather than Antolini's, that's really got Holden running. It should be obvious by now that I don't see *The Catcher in the Rye* as a coming-of-age story, especially not in the dismissive or pejorative sense; to me it's no more about the anxious life of an average teenager than *Huckleberry Finn* is. The feelings Salinger's trying to pinpoint don't really have much to do with the fluctuating moods of a representative teen; adolescence isn't the source of Holden's outsized feelings. Possibly because I came to the book as an adult, for me it's never been about the typical, but rather the exceptional; it's not meant to illustrate a phase of life we all pass through and share but instead to explore a disturbing and extreme loss of identity that leaves this one boy absolutely alone. And the depth of that loss comes from the fact that it's not directly his, but his family's. My guess is that in high school students learn that Holden doesn't go home right away because he knows he's going to be in big trouble. He's been kicked out of school again. He's failed and disappointed his parents once more, and his odyssey through New York is fueled by guilt and contrition. In my reading he doesn't go home after leaving Pencey because home is the problem. His real expulsion is from the family, not school, and his sojourn through New York renders that loss in literal terms: we see the resulting anomie, the thoroughness of his horror. Two very different engines drive the respective readings. In one, he's ultimately headed home, in the other he has nowhere to go, and never will.

Here's the assumption behind my guesswork. Suicide is a kind of death that makes you doubt what you know about the deceased or what you can ever know about anybody. It strikes clear to the core of identity, reaching down into the heart of your life. Since my brother died I haven't slept a single night alone with the lights off; I wake up afraid, and I have to know where I am, I need to see right away. And when I go out, I always leave a radio on, just so that when I come home I'll hear voices or, more precisely, I won't hear the silence and get all spooky imagining the surprises waiting for me. By a curious mechanism my brother's death has extended the vivid fears of my childhood into my adult life. I find that I'm alert in ways that adults don't need to be, and I'm ignorant of things grownups care most about. When a suicide happens within a family, that organism takes on the taint just as much as any individual. But that taint doesn't necessarily mean the dissolution of the family; it might have an opposite effect, banding the family together even tighter than before. (I felt like shameful secrets had been aired publicly, and I was first of all defensive, protec-

tive.) In reality, I think both things happen: you're pulled together, and that intense proximity exposes lines of cleavage that
had begun cracking years earlier. The suicide is just a piece finally falling out. And from then on the family story can't be the
same. Its identity must include death, a death shared in the
blood. The old narrative breaks at precisely the moment you
need it to speak for you. This death, this suicide, is shattering to
what, at that exact moment, is your deepest need—family, security, identity.

. . .

REREADING BUDDY'S STATEMENT about his ability to detect
authenticity, I find a harmonic floating just above the fundamental tone, and I think it can be heard distinctly in isolation
here:

> For the terrible and undiscountable fact has just
> reached me, between paragraphs, that I yearn to
> talk, to be queried, to be interrogated, about this
> particular dead man. *It's just got through to me,
> that apart from my many other—and, I hope to
> God, less ignoble—motives, I'm stuck with the
> usual survivor's conceit that he's the only soul alive
> who knew the deceased intimately.* [my italics]

This is the overtone you hear in Salinger's work, the know-
ingness, the high proud insistent certainty; and what accounts
for the sound—the instrument, so to speak—is the faculty of
mind that's meant to sift through supposed facts and separate
the truth from what's false; and the tone is this, the *belief* that

he alone holds the key, the final authentic word on the deceased (or any other matter). The emphasis here is on the belief, not the particular key, whatever it may be. (And I want to make clear that for me this is a musical sound as much as a matter of content. It's what makes *Raise High the Roof Beam, Carpenters* nearly unreadable for me—too much snotty all-knowing prep-school smugness in the prose, a vague assumption of values, a social vulgarity found in the rich and privileged that's just as revolting, and similar to, the arrogant know-nothingism of the various middle classes, upper to lower. Open the story to almost any page and you can hear the sound in the overpunctuated prose. It's as if the pissy aggrieved prose itself were defending Seymour. You can even hear a trace of the problem in the quote above, in the word "undiscountable"— the leftover locution of a kid putting on adult airs, afraid that someone will realize he doesn't know what he's talking about.) And so, if there really is a single truth, and you alone possess it, there is also, by definition, a lot of falseness out there—the bulk of life, in fact. And this construction, this arrangement or priority, pitting the defense of your holy truth against the entire world's falseness, is suicide refused, refused at least temporarily.

And it's silence refused, too.

Here's what I mean. A longstanding and widely accepted formulation is that suicide is redirected homicide. Edwin Shneidman, the father of the modern study of suicide, coined the phrase: "Suicide is murder in the 180th degree." There are variations on this, of course. Suicide's not always—probably never—an act of pure hostility. There's a fairly old article by

Ives Hendrick of the Harvard Medical School that argues the case for suicide as a form of identification with the lost love object, a fantasy of reunion rather than murder, and while this thinking doesn't occupy a place in the fat mainstream of suicidology, it is accepted, a tributary that helps explain some cases. I'm throwing these ideas out scattershot, hoping to indicate a central theme within the wide range of psychodynamic meanings attributed to suicide: that it's always accompanied by some shift away from life's normal priority, where it's perfectly natural and expected that you'd defend yourself from danger, to a condition where you give up, defenseless, or even join in on the attack. In Freud's still-fascinating "Mourning and Melancholia," he begins by openly admitting to being flummoxed by suicide and the self's attack on itself. He says the ego is usually fierce and robust in the protection of itself, rallying the troops when under siege, so how or why does ego-functioning break down and become defenseless in the suicide? In short, the self can only hate the self to the point of suicide when a lost internalized object—an object, moreover, of love—turns against the self. In other words, it's your inner daddy—protected by your love of him—messing with your defenseless inner child—or whatever, some variation of that. Later (1933), Karl Menninger develops his triadic theory of suicide—the wish to die, the wish to kill, the wish to be killed—to which, years afterward, he speculated on the need to add a fourth condition, the wish to be loved—and he talks about a mechanism by which the suicide's "hostile component, since it would otherwise have to be directed against the whole world, is turned inward upon the self." I'm really oversimplifying here, reducing

41

complex theories into these candied bits, and I'm skipping the work of so many, of Maltsberger, Hendin, Leenars, Jamison, etc., but I'm trying to get at something, this general tendency in suicide, that will bring us back to Salinger.

In suicide, then, a couple of the main poles of life flip, and the desire to talk or communicate turns into a longing for a colossal silence (most suicides don't write a note), and the fierce defense of the self becomes an equally fierce and final defeat. It's like the mind, exhausted by the enormous work of defending itself, turns around out of some need for efficiency or economy, and begins hating itself, doubting or attacking its reality. Being suicidal *is* really tiring. A lot of suicides are so lethargic and lacking in affect they aren't able to kill themselves until their mood improves—spring, for that reason, has the highest rate of what people in the business call "completed" suicides. The ego first tries to protect itself and then can't, in part because to do so would be to attack a forbidden love object. (Buddy Glass says he can't *finish* writing a description of Seymour, "even a bad description, even one where my ego, my perpetual lust to share top billing with him, is all over the place"—making a sideways admission of jealousy, and also expressing resentment for the sainted brother he can no longer defeat and no longer even describe without desecration.) What's salient in *The Catcher in the Rye* is that Holden achieves a fragile truce between hating himself and hating the world. Holden Caulfield is probably identified in the minds of most readers as a boy whose anger at and suspicion of the world is fragilely offset by his inviolate love for Allie and Phoebe. As long as he keeps that love immaculate, as long as he defends and protects it and maintains its purity, he's alive, and that's what I mean by suicide refused. Holden without his holy love is a goner, and the unalloyed quality of that love is really the register of his isolation. He's cornered, and you can see the gargantuan project he's set for himself, that vast defense. In the novel he ends up in an institution which isn't really a lasting solution to his problem but instead a sort of DMZ between himself and the world.

Similarly, Buddy Glass, a writer (in two other institutions, the military and the academy—and all these institutions, these supporting structures, stand in for a neutral family), asserts his identity by claiming close inner knowledge of his dead brother, Seymour. His relation to Seymour is sacerdotal and similar to the Holden Antolini says he can imagine dying nobly for an unworthy cause. But even in the passage quoted and italicized above, in the middle of his assertion, Buddy's already begun to undermine it, calling it a "conceit," an instance of cleverness that, but for the writer's vigilance, would have hardened into a fixed posture, would have become false, phony. And I would argue that only a little farther down this line of thinking we come to the idea that all writing, fixed on the page, claiming truth, is false. It's imaginable that a writer, in the wake of a suicide, might find all coherent narratives suspect, all postures false, and, looking at life up-close under a new magnifying hypervigilance, finally come to question and mistrust the integrity of his own inventions as well. The word "conceit" cancels Buddy's claim to know Seymour, dismissing it and sending it on its way toward silence. And silence—a kind of reunion with Seymour, or a way to equal or defeat him, head to head, silence for silence—is one possible response to this powerful but confused idea of falsity. If *The Catcher in the Rye* is noisy in its search for authenticity, then the rest of Salinger's work looks for the real by stilling the very engine that drives Holden's vast doubt—words. And this silence is related to and yet something beyond the interest in Zen quietude that crops up in Salinger's later work.

·   ·   ·

HOLDEN'S ISOLATION IN an institution as he tells his story points to a formal problem Salinger himself seems to have resolved through withdrawal and writerly silence. At least it's tempting to see it that way. I've poked around in all the work for prodromal clues somehow indicating Salinger's plunge into silence was symptomatic of something. What is the silence about? In some people (usually willful or grandiose or highly defended types) there's only a very small difference between talking incessantly and saying nothing. I vaguely remember a quote from Roland Barthes, who claimed his rhetorical needs alternated between a little haiku that expressed everything and a great flood of banalities that said nothing. And in *Seymour—An Introduction*, Buddy Glass says of his brother, "Vocally, he was either as brief as a gatekeeper at a Trappist monastery—sometimes for days, weeks at a stretch—or he was a non-stop talker." Interestingly, *The Catcher in the Rye*, Salinger's most *voluble* book, begins and ends with specific comments concerning what will *not* be written.

Holden starts his story with a refusal:

> If you really want to hear about it, the first thing
> you'll probably want to know is where I was born,
> and what my lousy childhood was like, and how

my parents were occupied and all before they had
me, and all that David Copperfield kind of crap, but
I don't feel like going into it, if you want to know
the truth.

And he ends the novel with this hardened commandment:

"Don't ever tell anybody anything. If you do, you
start missing everybody."

The quotes above bracket the book, suggesting prohibitions of both point of view and content. Holden will not look at the life of his parents or take the tack of examining his past or childhood—this is no remembrance—and by the end of the novel his instinct, in a sense, proves him right, proves that the process of writing only creates further problems. He's not newly wise like Nick Carraway. He has no new perspective or understanding. The only thing Holden seems to learn from telling even this restricted story is that, confirming his first hunch, it would have been better to say nothing.

Silence is already there, waiting in the wings of Salinger's most clamorous and fluent book.

Is silence for a writer tantamount to suicide? In some ways it is, I believe, but the question for me is why—why does the writer choose silence? The deliberate decision to quit clawing at the keyboard is too mechanical to be an answer. Stopping isn't the real matter, but rather the result of some other prior disturbance that can't be named. Silence in this sense isn't the equivalent of suicide or death, but of secrecy. That's what it's about—what is *not* said. Taking Salinger's oeuvre as a unified field, I find a couple elements that don't square with either my experience or my avocational reading in the literature of suicide—elements where a silence rules. He never really looks at the role of parents in family life, and never examines, in particular, their position re. Seymour's suicide. It's a substantial omission, and perhaps not an omission at all but instead a protective silence. I don't know, and on this point I don't care to speculate beyond the observation that, in general, people from good, functioning families rarely kill themselves. And in crappy, broken-down familes a child's attention is often focused on nothing but the parents. Suffice it to say there's something big missing in Salinger's account. And the other thing not present in Salinger's work is outright anger toward Seymour or a sense of doubt about him. As Buddy describes him, Seymour really has no flaws at all, and to me this absence of flaws and of anger and doubt is a texture that's conspicuously absent. Why? I can't say, although I feel the effects. In *Seymour—An Introduction* Buddy never lets the reader forget that he, Buddy, is sitting alone at his desk, writing. It's all just writing, he wants us to know, the lumber of it, the cut and stacked phrases, the punctuation nailed to the paper, the parentheses put up to frame different doubts, etc.—as if to say this project, this monument under construction, will always fall short of honoring the actual character. Where Holden insists on Phoebe's innocence and pretty easily posits an idea of her essence, Buddy sees past his brother into the conceits and constructions that create him on the page. And because of this, perhaps, Seymour never feels real, never seems to emerge from the workbench of the writer, to live and walk among men.

The writer won't or can't let him die:

> What I am, I think, is a thesaurus of undetached
> prefatory remarks about him. I believe I essentially
> remain what I've almost always been—a narrator,
> but one with extremely pressing personal needs. I
> want to introduce, I want to describe, I want to dis-
> tribute momentos, amulets, I want to break out my
> wallet and pass around snapshots, I want to follow
> my nose.

Here again you get a kind of intense identification with
Seymour, one that blocks Buddy's way—he's "undetached," he
has "pressing personal needs," and because of this he can only
make "prefatory" remarks. The isolated *I am* is telling; with
the comma where it is, the weight of the sentence remains stuck
to the subject, rather than shifting forward via the verb to its
object. The *I am* seems open-ended, perpetual. (Is time taken
out of the sentence because the writer won't let history happen,
won't let his character die? It's curious that in a life that's
ended, that's so emphatically finished, the writer can't begin,
can't offer anything more than an introduction. Would finishing Seymour mean outliving him? Or the converse: does failing
to finish Seymour leave him alive?) The identity thing here is
ruthless, close, smothering, endless. Consider that quote and
the problem when set beside this:

> . . . I privately say to you, old friend (unto you,
> really, I'm afraid), please accept from me this

unpretentious bouquet of very early-blooming parentheses: (((( )))). I suppose, most unflorally. I truly mean them to be taken, first off, as bow-legged—buckle-legged—omens of my state of mind and body at this writing.

There's that cowardly, obfuscating "un-" construction—*unpretentious, unflorally*—cropping up again (which nearly always works as a mask, sneaky and meaning the very opposite of what it states; meaning, in this case, pretentious, floral), but the point now is to draw attention to the parentheses. (Although in working through various drafts of this essay I realized my second paragraph was full of precisely this construction. It appears five times, and occupies the priveleged key position as the last word in the paragraph. It crossed my mind to correct the problem by burying it in some low geological stratum of the piece, but I haven't. There's that desire in writing, as in life, to rewind everything after a suicide, to return to some pristine moment, and so in this, too, Salinger's *mon frere, ma semblable*.) The parentheses sit like Kevlar jackets all through the writing, protecting Buddy's identity from attack, keeping the sentences safe. *Seymour—An Introduction* is like a story in hiding, its prose on the lam, its characters putting on disguises, its ideas concealed. The whole thing is preambular, it's all excursus, and it's a bad sign that for me the best or most accurate language for describing the story comes from classical rhetoric and oratory. The sentences spin eloquently over an absence—it's as if progress has stopped, and the last few words are draining out. Earlier I said that Holden is making a loud shouted appeal directly to the audience, over the heads of those who don't understand. The whole story is directed at you, the reader. In *Seymour* Buddy Glass speaks directly to the reader too, but now he resorts to the aside, the isolated whispered phrase, safely enclosed in parentheses, addressing the *audience* in a low voice supposedly *inaudible* to others nearby.

Who is nearby?

I know: his brother.

. . .

SALINGER ISN'T PRIMARILY a funny writer, and humor, except sporadically in *The Catcher in the Rye*, is largely absent from his work. His primary thing is empathy, the yearning for it, the hope and the need, both as giver and receiver. Buddy's desire for empathic union with his brother is single-minded and loyal and makes for an interesting case, but Seymour never finally comes to life. The book is a one long stutter and a fascinating failure. Buddy can't write Seymour because, when he tries, Seymour fragments and falls apart—you get the parts, you get the eyes, the nose, the voice, etc. He wants his brother so bad, it's a sad thing to watch, to see Seymour breaking to pieces in Buddy's hands. The Salinger I've been discussing seems at times to feel he's got a corner on The Truth, this unwieldy lump he keeps hidden like the kid with the secret goldfish in D.B.'s story, who won't show it to anybody because he bought it with his own money. Perhaps this Truth is centrally important because the suicide takes his secret with him, and it's easy to get caught up in a monomaniacal search for The Answer, pinning your painfully vast hope to a single Idea. Up to a point, you believe the person who killed himself took the ultimate truth, and life afterward often feels like a sorrowful search for that last, unknown key to the life, which will explain everything. The paradox is that this hope or need for certainty seems to make the world less stable. The belief in a single Truth leads to doubt about everything. The need for empathic union makes the actual separation just terribly, terribly huge.

When we shift the relationship away from Buddy-Seymour to Salinger-Holden, then, as an act of writing, Salinger's empathy for Holden Caulfield makes *The Catcher in the Rye* something special, an intense and fierce and intimate look at a character who arouses in readers—in me, let's say—a level of sympathetic identification nearly equal to the one felt for Fitzgerald's Gatsby.

After my brother's death I felt I had too much feeling to be myself. I felt attacked by my emotions, under siege, and the sensation, day after day, was like life had stuck to me. Like it was pinned to my back. This whatever, this stab of feeling, probably influenced the fate of the doomed robin. I could have stood by until the crow killed it, or sat still until somebody a little more altruistic came down the street and stepped in to save it, rushing the bird off to a Humane Society shelter; or someone else could have come down the street, this time in a car, and run it over. Lots of things could have happened. But instead, I scooped the bird up in my Filson cap, folding the hat like a taco shell so it couldn't escape, and carried it to a vacant lot with a weedy path that led down to the lake. For some reason I thought the crow might follow us, but crows are comical birds and that one's interest had already moved on to something new. I walked into the murky water of Lake Union, my mind blank, and, bending down, dunked the hat under. The bird was still trying to fly, brushing its one good wing against the fabric, and when that stopped I pulled my hat away. The robin floated to the surface, lifelessly riding the tiny waves, and I smacked the hat against my leg, knocking beads of water off the waxed cotton. I picked a few gray feathers from the inner brim and put the hat on, looking west across the water to the Aurora Bridge. And while now the bridge reminds me of my brother Mike, comically pratfalling through an indifferent universe, back then it made me think of Danny, tragically dead at twenty-one after shooting himself in my bedroom.

With Danny, years have passed and I still feel a deathly guilt. I never did anything but love my brother and that wasn't enough. And now every breath I take is a betrayal, a refusal of his choice. It's not sentimental indulgence, it's not so much that I ask myself what happened to the hand I held in crosswalks, but rather that I cross all those streets again. I stay with him now, I'm *always* nearby. I am always ten and he is always three, and I sit in the kitchen spooning canned peas into his mouth, swallowing most of them myself, and he gets a bowl of spumoni for being a good boy and eating his vegetables. I'm with him and I never feel like I belong entirely to present-day life. I've never really held a serious job or applied myself to anything worthwhile, I'm an unreliable, shitty friend, and I've never loved anyone deeply or satisfactorily. Killing the robin was an early experiment in grieving and acceptance that didn't work too well. I knew the bird had no life ahead of it, and I wanted to anticipate that doom rather than stand off at a safe distance. I didn't want to be uncertain. But where before I had too much feeling, after drowning the bird I felt nothing, I was indifferent, I was remorseless. I thought I could rejoin the universe by being cruel and unfeeling, but obviously I was having trouble with focal distance and zeroing in on the exact right place where most of life was happening.

Here is a quote from Dietrich Bonhoeffer that I treasure for capturing one side of how I feel. It gets me closer to acceptance and understanding than anything else. It's from his *Letters & Papers from Prison*, and written, I think, at a time when he knew he would die in the concentration camp, so he speaks from inside the heart of his death:

> Nothing can make up for the absence of someone whom we love, and it would be wrong to try to find a substitute; we must simply hold out and see it through. That sounds very hard at first, but at the same time it is a great consolation, for the gap, as long as it remains unfulfilled, preserves the bonds between us. It is nonsense to say that God fills the gap. God doesn't fill it, but on the contrary, keeps it empty and so helps us to keep alive our former communion with each other, even at the cost of pain.

From the get-go, my brother Mike's suicide attempt struck me as a piece of comedy. Maybe that's because it came to me like the comedian's idea of the topper, the rule that says you follow up a good joke with a second, even better joke. Keep them laughing! Maybe it's because I always picture Mike tumbling haplessly through space, and falls are a staple of comedy and clowning, as is anything that turns the body into an object. Maybe it's because when he jumped over the rail he was being chased by the devil and then he was aware, halfway down, that the devil was gone and he was all alone, falling like a rock. Or maybe, as in *King Lear*, it's just too much, and the wise man sees life like the fool and laughs, either that or he cracks. Mike was really wrecked-up, his body broken, and when I saw him at the VA hospital he had nuts and bolts and this kind of light-gauge medical rebar rising like a scaffolding from his smashed pelvis. His right shoulder was immobilized, so that, in combination with the broken pelvis, and his ruined bladder, which was being drained by a catheter, he seemed like just another malfunctioning contraption or a Rube Goldberg contrivance. At home we always had old jalopy equipment like black and white televisions with no horizontal hold and our cars were ancient and unreliable and broken-down—in one of our cars the transmission would overheat and the carpet in the backseat would catch fire and smolder on any drive longer than ten miles, so we did the obvious thing, we kept a jug of water in the car. In the hospital Mike looked to me just like another one of our crappy busted things, where the attempt at repair was funny in a way that the initial problem was not. Whereas I remember helping Danny eat his peas, I remember laughing at Mike as he tried to get a hamburger to his mouth. I sat in a chair and watched. He couldn't do it—you can't sit up straight with a broken pelvis—and his mouth and the hamburger just hung there, apart from each other, it seemed, for all time.

And so over here, Henri Bergson's essay on the comic suggests another side, a possible path for me in my ongoing attempt to understand life by reading books:

> . . . I would point out . . . the absence of feeling which usually accompanies laughter. . . . In-

difference is its natural environment, for laughter has no greater foe than emotion. . . . In a society composed of pure intelligences there would probably be no more tears, though perhaps there would still be laughter; whereas highly emotional souls, in tune and unison with life, in whom every event would be sentimentally prolonged and re-echoed, would neither know nor understand laughter.

Put in a slightly different way, it was Charlie Chaplin, I think, who said that life up-close is a tragedy, but from a distance it's a comedy. Somebody slipping on a banana peel is still funny, unless it's you. And the genius of Salinger is that, speaking through Holden Caulfield, highly emotional, in tune and unison with life, with events re-echoing still, he told us exactly what it feels like to feel too much.

Salinger's Daughter: Whining Bitch
(Or "How I Became the Voice of Youth")

EMMA FORREST

I slept with J.D. Salinger when I was fourteen. We did it in a day. He told me that I was the most beautiful, the most special, and so misunderstood. By nightfall, I was done with him. I was horrified, not long after, to discover that there were other people, mostly young people, just as beautiful, special and misunderstood as I.

I put him out of my mind. Fickle teenage girl that I was, J.D. was just another case of romantic mistaken identity: "Him, him, and only him. I'll die if he doesn't need me. Hang on . . . Nope, my mistake, not him at all. Send it back, please." I did the same to Jack Kerouac the summer before. And, although it was I who discarded him, and although his presence in the bedrooms of my girlfriends irked me more than I can say, J.D. Salinger did get me my first job. Three years after sleeping with *The Catcher in the Rye* under my pillow, *The Times* of London hired me as their teenage columnist. I wrote about politics and pop culture from the "point of view of a young person."

The young person they expected me to be had been "invented" in the fifties by the two J.D.'s—Salinger and James Dean. The concept of teenagers, rather than mini-adults, did not exist before then. Forty-five years later, I was being paid to encapsulate—in six hundred words a week—youth as defined by a dead homosexual and an old man with a proclivity for young girls. A man who might as well be dead.

I didn't know any teenagers. I had never even kissed a teenage boy. I had barely even talked to one. I left my all-girls school the second I got my column. I didn't like young people and I didn't like their cinema, literature, or records. I was an old curmudgeon who sequestered herself in her bedroom with her mother's Joni Mitchell albums. The "young" people I was supposed to appeal to could, I'm sure, see through me a mile off. But my column seemed to fascinate "grownups," as though I were decoding a secret language for them.

I was in a no-man's-land, without friends my own age, and disliked by many of my adult colleagues. Yet I didn't know how to interact with anyone but adults, and worshiped my parents' friends and icons. I mentioned a film actor in my column, one of the seminal British stars of the sixties. He wrote me a letter saying that if his hair weren't so silver he'd invite me to tea. I told him his silver hair was my favorite thing about him. I was sixteen. He was in his fifties. He didn't touch me. One day, as I was climbing out of a swimming pool in California, he kissed my cheek, my forehead, then my mouth. I didn't know if I was being seduced or anointed.

I realized, when a section editor called me into his office to talk about how I might contribute to his supplement, then tried to get me to sit on his knee, that J.D. had set me up. J.D. Salinger is the literary equivalent of a pedophile: the child's world equals good, and all adults are fake and phony. That's how a pervert thinks. It's no surprise, perusing her memoirs, to find that as a sixteen-year-old, Joyce Maynard looked all of twelve. By the age of fifteen I already knew that "Teenage" was not a place of original sinless purity, but a chaos of hormonal imbalance. Was I a unicorn with acne, as they would have me believe, or just a stripper exploiting the well-paying punter? Although the men I worked with eyed me like some mythical beast—a real live teenager in the office!—I felt like the latter.

Ever since the publication of *The Catcher in the Rye*, newspapers and magazines have sought to employ a voice of youth. There were several before me and several after, a revolving door of hormone-addled James Bonds, dropping non sequiturs with eyebrows visibly cocked, even in print. The Sean Connery of young newspaper columnists was Julie Burchill, who, at age sixteen, answered an advert in the back of *New Musical Express*.

The weekly music inky was looking for "hip young gunslingers." They hired Burchill, who, having applied on lined paper torn from a school exercise book, became the very first person to write about the Sex Pistols. She knew that Johnny Rotten's big put-down was "You're too old." When he knelt at her feet she duly asked him his age. "Nineteen," he stammered. "You're too old," sneered Burchill.

With the publication of "Generation X," it was Douglas Coupland's turn to be labeled the voice of youth, and Julie

Burchill, by then in her thirties, threw a dinner in his honor. She placed me by her side and referred to me as "Jailbait" and "Gym-slip" all night, palpably relieved that she was no longer the literary Lolita. Coupland invited me and my friend Richey—a beauteous, self-mutilating British rock star; since missing, presumed dead—back to his hotel and asked us about young people. What were our likes and dislikes? Richey batted his giant kohl-rimmed eyes and stirred his vodka orange with a black varnished nail. We couldn't answer.

In the very first page of *Catcher*, Holden Caulfield dismisses "all that David Copperfield kind of crap." Sure Copperfield was a teen, so was Pip, so were many other characters, and yet we never consider them such—they are young adults, existing before Salinger's romantification of the teen. Once Salinger came along, people wondered for the first time if the teenager knew something they didn't. It became standard for young authors—myself included—who really weren't ready to be published, to be signed too soon and never cultivated. In Europe, the past few years alone have seen the publication of under-baked novels by Bidisha, Rebecca Ray, Caitlin Moran, and Benjamin Leibert. The only really great "adolescent" novel is *Sarah* by J.T. Leroy, who is earthy without ever being earthbound, a child of Dickens rather than Salinger. In the mighty shadow of *Sarah*, we read like a bunch of Tiny Tim's just about remembering to say "Ow, my leg hurts" when we can be bothered.

I don't like the columns I wrote, or my first novel. I came of age as a member of a generation that had no significant gap with the establishment, no punk, hippie, or beat. There was no secret language to be cracked and so the columns were mostly just padding. "You're stealing my culture," Dad would sigh, walking in on me as I wept to Joni Mitchell's *Blue*. To the bemusement of my editors, I'd often turn in columns about why Randy Newman was great. "Don't you have anything of your own?" Mum would ask, as I settled in for a Monty Python marathon. I see now that I was experiencing the Bob/Jakob Dylan dichotomy: how can the child of a maverick create work that is anything other than conservative in comparison? Indeed, why should he try to?

I felt sure that, as we neared the end of the millennium, everything was in its right place. The best song had been written, the best film had been made, the best beauty encased in it. So Oasis were the new Beatles, Blur the new Kinks, Russell Crowe the reincarnation of Richard Burton. Rose McGowan and Marilyn Manson were Ava Gardner and Frank Sinatra. I still believe that there are a finite number of musical notes and that only the tonality can change. That year, as every year since 1951, each publishing house had at least one novel a season listed in the catalog as the best writing on teenagers since *The Catcher in the Rye*. Because of my Caulfield-esque column, I was approached to write one myself. I felt no shame in being marketed as the next Salinger. In retrospect, I wish I had ripped off someone more talented.

It is entirely possible to be original without being very good. Salinger, whilst an innovator, is not really a writer. Looking back at *Catcher*, the prose is workmanlike at best. It's relentlessly middle class, middlebrow and tremendously unchallenging. Yes, he captured something special, but he did it without writing that well. As compared to, say, William Faulkner, who broke new ground with use of the interior monologue, or Truman Capote, where the writing is such a pleasure, like listening to music, J.D. Salinger never dances. His success is in pulling you into the character of Holden Caulfield—and that is a great success—but the prose itself is never elevating or thrilling the way *Goodbye, Columbus* would be ten years later.

Ten years after first reading it, I don't relate to Holden Caulfield. I don't like him. I don't feel that people who are phony are necessarily a bad thing. When I think of all the phonies that I have loved who have, as Kurt Vonnegut wrote, lived by "the harmless untruths" that make them "healthy and happy"—or as Courtney Love sang, "fake it so real"—they are "beyond fake." Courtney, Madonna, Truman Capote, Gore Vidal, Rex Reed, David Bowie, Quentin Crisp, any rap star you care to mention, Katharine Hepburn, Rosalind Russell, Grace Kelly, Bette Davis—all those Golden Age of Hollywood actresses with English accents!—Audrey Hepburn, the phoniest and most delightful of them all. Phoniness is what kept me afloat as a teenager. Airs and graces, double lives, pretense and pretentiousness, are about the only things a sixteen-year-old girl has to live for.

In American culture these days, the female teenager wants nothing to do with Holden Caulfield, the beta male who knows he can never be an alpha and retreats, like Mark Chapman, into terrible thoughts because of this unassailable conundrum. The female teenager is Amy Fisher, Monica Lewinsky, this confidence, this sexuality that has the power to bring down car mechanics or presidents. Teen female sexuality can literally threaten the stability of the Western world. Teen male sexuality threatens only the interior landscape of the tortured individual.

J.D. Salinger is that self-loathing beta, idolizing his little sister, idolizing childhood, so afraid of not succeeding that he had to retreat completely in case he failed. Reading his work as a twenty-four-year old, I fully understand his decision. Philip Roth's American trilogy of the last decade is the best work of his career. Salinger could never have done that. He simply wasn't good enough.

I told you, when I was fourteen I loved him for that day, and I meant it. But, looking back, I know that he wasn't the best but merely the first. "I'm leaving now," he said dramatically, and we remember him as far more impressive than he really was. The best thing about the way he flounced out of that room is that he didn't come back. He gets to live the ultimate teenage fantasy of being able to watch your own funeral and getting to see how much everyone misses you.

Me, Rebecca Ray, Julie Burchill, Bret Easton Ellis, Douglas Coupland, Susanna Kaysen, Molly Jong-Fast—we were all fucked by Salinger. He never rang, he wouldn't return our calls, and he didn't even acknowledge our presence. He left no scent on the pillow. He wasn't even that good in bed. But he did get all of us our jobs.

The Importance of
Wax and Olives

ALEKSANDER HEMON

I.

I have a cousin, Natasha, who is a lovely young lady living in
Edmonton, Canada, today, and whose latest ambition is to be a
(super)model. When she was a little girl we got along splen-
didly, largely because I was one of the few adults (I was in my
late teens) who had patience for the rapid fire of her questions.
Her questions were uniformly tricky and clever. Once she asked
me: "Who do you love more? Me or poisonous snakes?" What
killed me was the plural "poisonous snakes." I would have
chosen her over a single harmless snake, no problem, but she
was the exact opposite of the poisonous plurality, and she knew
it. Her questions were tricky mainly because she always knew
the answers—she asked her cousins and aunts and uncles (I am
technically her uncle) questions simply to see if they knew the
answers, and they almost never did. Once, as we were spitting

out cherry pits as far as we could, she asked me: "Why does it snow?" I, of course, had a general idea, but what I knew was what I learned in my high-school physics classes, which I mainly spent reading books under the desk (unless the class was devoted to the theory of relativity), so my answer featured atmosphere, condensation, moisture, pressure differences, etc., and it sounded very complicated, contrived, and glaringly untrue. She simply said: "No!" I could not think of a simple way to explain it, and my already shaky feeling of adult competence was melting by the moment under the gaze of the choir of aunts and uncles, who had unwisely considered me intelligent. In panic, skillfully assuming a condescending attitude of a know-it-all adult, I asked her back: "Do you know why it snows?" And she simply answered: "Because it is cold," which, naturally, was the simplest and the most obvious of truths—the connection between cold and snow was unmediated, it was what it was.

I think of my little cousin every time I read, and I do it regularly, the great Salinger story "A Perfect Day for Bananafish," in which the following exchange between the little girl named Sybil and the young man named Seymour takes place:

"Do you like wax?" Sybil asked.

"Do I like what?" asked the young man.

"Wax."

"Very much. Don't you?"

Sybil nodded. "Do you like olives?" she asked.

"Olives—yes. Olives and wax. I never go any place without 'em."

Sybil's interest in wax and olives is not a matter of innocence or cuteness—for one thing, she likes to chew candles—but rather of a need to know things *as they are*. Her questions are an expression of a desire to understand them in a state before they enter a web of social evaluations and hierarchies, before science and analysis, before wax is considered a worthless, formless thing, useless unless it is a candle, before olives are accessories to a martini—before, if you wish, they become commodities. Salinger's kids and young adolescents always have a profound interest in things whose true value is well below—indeed beyond—their use value, let alone their market value. They simply like certain things, regardless of how valuable or worthless they might be for the rest of the world; recall Holden Caulfield's red hunting cap, determinedly uncool, or his brother's baseball mitt, which becomes a topic of Stradlater's English paper, not too valuable to be shared, even with a phony stud.

Moreover, Salinger characters have interest in things and people no one else seems to care about. Among the heady answers that Holden pursues on his Manhattan peregrinations is the question of the Central Park ducks, which he discusses with a cabbie named Horwitz:

> "Hey, Horwitz," I said. "You ever pass by the lagoon
> in Central Park? Down by Central Park South?"
> "The *what*?"
> "The lagoon. That little lake, like, there. Where the
> ducks are. You know?"
> "What about it?"
> "Well, you know the ducks that swim around in it?

In the springtime and all? Do you happen to know where they go in the wintertime, by any chance?"

"Where *who* goes?"

"The ducks. Do you know, by any chance? I mean does somebody come around in a truck or something and take them away, or do they fly away by themselves—go south or something?"

Old Horwitz turned all the way around and looked at me. He was a very impatient-type guy. He wasn't a bad guy, though. "How the hell should I know?" he said. "How the hell should I know a stupid thing like that?"

The question of the ducks is representative of all the questions in Salinger's novels, and perhaps the world at large, regarding the destiny of irrelevant things, things that get lost in the whirlwinds of history, mindless consumption and general phoniness. My sister always worried about the horses in westerns: they would be shot under John Wayne or fall down under the Indians, and they would disappear from the picture. She always wanted to know what happened next to the horses in movies, and she could never find an answer, for horses don't matter, they just come and go. History, currently mostly serving people who benefit from mindless consumption, much too often functions like a western: the great heroic Man in the center, embodying this or that great idea, armed with a mighty rifle and a firm belief in Law, as Indians and horses, insufficiently important, disappear from the picture. So do the ducks, for that matter, as it is rather reasonable to assume that Holden Caulfield never found out, and that he, when he became a man, either lost interest in the ducks, which would indicate phoniness, or he became an unaccommodated, miserable man, committing suicide like Seymour Glass, who had not only lost the ability to value wax and olives, but knew it.

Taking an interest in unimportant things and irrelevant questions is a useful strategy for a writer—for what is literature if not the history of disappearable things and insufficiently historic(al) people. Salinger is a master of the memorable detail, the seemingly random gesture, the debris of mundane daily operations, the stuff that is left out of any analysis. Alfred Kazin noted, in an instance of wishful analytical thinking, that "someday there will be learned theses on *The Use of Ashtray in J.D. Salinger's Stories*; no other writer has made so much of Americans lighting up, reaching for the ashtray, setting up the ashtray with one hand while with the other they reach for a ringing telephone." The mind of a Salinger character is not rendered by a stream of consciousness, but by a stream of body motions and random objects that form his or her perceptual universe.

All of Salinger can fit in Bessie Glass's pockets containing "two or three packs of cigarettes, several match folders, a screwdriver, a claw-end hammer, a Boy Scout knife that had once belonged to one of her sons, and an enamel faucet handle or two, plus an assortment of screws, nails, hinges, and ball-bearing casters"; or in "a soggy, collapsed castle" that Sybil sinks her foot in. All those marvelous, *invaluable* things and details, along with Sybil's wax and olives, easily bring to mind the well-known Zen story, doubtless dear to old J.D., in which a Zen master is asked what is the most valuable thing in the world. "A dead cat's head," he answers, "because no one could put a price on it." The Zen story is specifically invoked in the story *Raise High the Roof Beam, Carpenters*, as Seymour in his diary recalls explaining to his fiancée, Muriel, the remark he had made at the dinner table, about wanting to be "a dead cat," which thereafter haunted Muriel's mother for weeks.

For Salinger, children are the only people in the world who can effortlessly understand the true value of a dead cat and wax and olives. This knowledge, this *wisdom*—the word that has vanished in the age of information—stems from the direct, presumably unmediated, contact with the world; from the ability to grasp, with their hands, things "as they are." *Things as they are* is a slippery phrase, if not an ontological nonsense, but I think that when talking about Salinger the category of *things as they are* simply means things with no particular essence separate from their material presence in the world, with no transcendence or spiritual dimension, things that don't need to be thought about or analyzed to be comprehended or known—they simply *are*. The mystical essence of a thing, something that is inside it and that one tries to possess for moot metaphysical reasons—rather than the thing itself—is the first symptom of that thing being a commodity. For a commodity to enter the market and attain a value as a thing alienated from human labor, it cannot be an empty thing—it cannot just be a material object. It has to be greater than itself, it has to fulfill a need that is not merely material—it must have a spiritual essence that responds to a spiritual need. The essence is inserted by the discourse of self-expression through consumption, and the material use value is displaced by the phantom spiritual value: the driverless SUV—rather than just being a thing that transports you from A to B—climbs steep mountainsides for no discernible reason, other than wanting to go higher and higher, symbolizing a soaring human spirit; and the sneakers—not merely shoes—that make you *just do it* (though what *it* might be is hard to tell) represent spiritual self-confidence, the *with-it-ness* easily attainable in the local Nike superstore. To possess, to own that essence, that ineffable quality of a commodity that differentiates it from other commodities, one has to buy the thing that contains it, which makes one different from those who buy those other commodities. Consumption spiritualizes and individualizes the consumer, as he or she enters a web of imaginary relations between human beings and the world. And the essence cannot be captured, as it is fundamentally unreal, which is convenient enough for an endless pursuit; the pursuit of happiness is the pursuit of imaginary metaphysical goodies, frequently lodged within an affordable, fantastically beautiful commodity.

On the other hand, *things as they are*, whose essence is nothing, is a concept fundamental to Zen Buddhism, in which the essence of the Buddha himself is nothing.[1] Children are natural Zen masters for Salinger, as they are able to bypass the mirage of essences and access things as material, *real* objects. Children know things, not their essences. What is in question here is not the "innocence" of children, but their total presence in this world and their real connection to it. Salinger believes

---

1. This concept of the Buddha as nothing is what a particular kind of poetry, typified by haiku, is founded on. That kind of poetry has long been shot to hell in this country, after decades of the dominance of confessional poetry and the related bourgeois metaphysics, steadily and mercilessly perpetuated in creative writing programs. That kind of poetry is what Buddy Glass appreciates, along with his cranky car-mates in *Raise High the Roof Beam, Carpenters*, when Buddy's deaf and dumb childlike friend writes, "in letters that had not quite jelled yet, the single word 'Delighted.' "

that if one is to know the world and oneself, one needs to know one's wax and olives. The tag of "innocence" is, of course, condescending, as children are never clean slates without desires and complicated relations with the world and people around them. I remember that as a child I always knew more than the adults thought I did, and pretending to be an "innocent" child got me out of many a dire situation. And every child I knew did the same thing—pretty often adults seemed to be a little slow and somewhat unconscious. But besides being condescending, "innocence" always implies a need for protection and guidance—in one word, control.

In this country, children are brought up by their loving parents (and armies of interested groups and agencies run by politicians' spouses) to be good citizens and consumers. Their "innocence" needs to be protected from sexual predators, from the omnipresent sex and violence, from a collection of harmful syndromes, or from the general lack of support from their parents. Children are nurtured by a frightful mechanism of control which never, not even for a moment, leaves them alone to handle the world without the mediation of power, to access *things as they are*—bringing up children means training them to be consumers, to believe in the unreal. Their lack of interest in commodities is taken to be cute idiocy, i.e. "innocence." I remember going to see a Disney movie with a friend of mine and her three-year-old son. He lost any interest in the movie within fifteen minutes or so and proceeded to play with a straw. Meanwhile, behind our back a little girl was wailing, begging her mother. "Please don't make me watch this! Please don't make me watch this stupid movie!" And her mother kept saying: "Just watch it. You'll like it." The girl apparently didn't know, in her "innocence," that she was supposed to like Disney movies, because all children are supposed to like them—provided that they were not tainted by some evil cultural spell. Fortunately, she did not give up—she had a powerful voice, and her mother finally took her out of the theater. I hope she is somewhere away from the Disney nurturing, exploring wax and olives.

The acculturation of children, their training to be obedient consumers and good citizens ("Just watch it, you'll like it" equally applies to Disney movies and American democracy), is contingent upon their alleged idiotic "innocence." The underlying assumption is that unless they are told, children know nothing and are susceptible to all kinds of vile influences. According to the discourse of "innocence," children are at the bottom of the ladder of consciousness, and with careful parental and societal guidance they might reach the coveted top—where a fifty-year-old white intellectual, divorced from the practice of life and his wife, Herzog Unbound himself,[2] is perched, steadily uncoiling threads for the all-encompassing net of bourgeois metaphysics, while fretting feminist conspiracies and bemoaning the decay of civilization.

Salinger's greatest asset, I think, is his *respect* for children and the interest in the world that he shares with them. His eye is directed toward the detail that is not visible to the acculturated, properly trained adults, who are much too mired in their

---

2. In a 1963 interview, Saul Bellow dismissed Salinger as "an excellent craftsman" but one who "has made up a Rousseauian critique of society which comes from the vatic judgment of the immature, as though civilization were something from which youth had the privilege of withdrawing and into which they have particular insights not available to others."

petty metaphysics, or devoted to tracking down the child within themselves in order to control it. When I was a child, I remember always being close to the ground: I saw the things that were on the ground, from cigarette butts to cracks in the pavement. As I grew, I moved away from the ground, though I have clear memories of the pavement in front of the building I grew up in. And I formed attachments to useless things: once I spent a summer at my grandparents' attached to a wooden stick, crooked in just the right way. What I like about Salinger is that he values the things that I learned as a child to be important, things like wax and olives, which also require a particular way of looking at the world—sideways, like a child violinist—for such things are always out of the picture.

II.

Here comes the hard part: I have to confront Salinger's shortcomings and shortsightedness. That ain't easy, because I still clearly remember the copy of *The Catcher in the Rye* I checked out of a Sarajevo library and never returned. I was fifteen or so. Its soft cover was reinforced by a plastic wrapping, which became sticky in the many hands that held it (it was the only copy in that library), and its pages were thin with flipping. I started speaking like Holden Caulfield (in translation), ignoring my school reading assignments (*The Old Man and the Sea*, a book about an old man floating on a sea of pretentious boredom) and proudly informing my teacher that I was reading Salinger, which, come to think of it, did not surprise her at all. What I am trying to say is that, with those heavy coffers of nostalgia banging against my ankles, it is hard to stay straight on the unsentimental critical path (as may well be clear from Part 1 of this essay), but I must try.

Here is, then, the basic Salinger problem: children grow up, it is biologically inescapable. The Zen talents of children, or their "vatic" properties, are likely to get lost as they enter adulthood—wax and olives won't do any longer. "Anybody over sixteen without an ulcer's a goddam spy," Zooey Glass announces to Franny—the sentiment is understandable, but also recognizably unrealistic and untenable. Though some of us carry the burden of the thought that we used to be really smart and clear-sighted as children and that it's all been down-hill from there, to dismiss adulthood as an absolute domain of phoniness is just, well, much too simple. Besides, the phony adulthood that is Salinger's nightmare is a particular kind of adulthood: middle-class, white, Manhattanite, Ivy League. The ultimate phonies are Yale graduate students (detecting a Yale phony is shooting fish in the graduate barrel), like Lane Coutell, Franny's boyfriend; or Dick Hess, the TV writer, an "out-of-towner" in New York; or Luce, Holden's ex-advisor, a Columbia student who is dating "a sculpture babe" from Shanghai and happens to find "Eastern philosophy more satis-factory than Western." ("Whaddya mean 'philosophy'?" Holden asks. "Ya mean sex and all?") The targets are much too easy, and more importantly, just a philosophical slip away from Holden or Zooey or Franny (who nearly slides into the vortex of Yale phoniness). The phonies are people who, like a cen-tipede in a Zen story, think about which leg to move first—or, even worse, enjoy moving one leg at a time, enjoy their wan-dering off the path to nirvana. The non–Ivy League, non–Manhattan people, the people who can't afford the leisure to choose between Eastern or Western philosophy, they never enter Salinger's picture. Spirituality, including its phony forms, is a class privilege.

Salinger's alternative to the all-devouring phoniness is the fictional Glass family, easily the most utopian family in the history of American fiction. The Glass children, precocious as they are, have all been participants in a radio show called "It's a Wise Child," and have been exposed to a thorough religious-philosophical education, concocted by Seymour and Buddy, their eldest brothers. As is the case with many utopian projects, the Glass family never quite works out—there is the darkness of Seymour's suicide and younger brother Walt's absurd death (a gas stove exploded) at its center. Seymour is a particularly interesting case, for it seems that he became the philosophical master of the Glass family on his own. Seymour seems to be self-educated. He just followed his childish Zen path, never succumbing to the temptations of phoniness, even if it had the innocent face and the attractive body of Muriel, his fiancée and then his wife. Yet, it didn't help him. In fact it did him in. The question is—and it's a reasonable one—whether spirituality is supposed to *help* at all, rather than *enlighten*. And enlightenment does not exclude suicide. The troubling part is that Seymour arguably imposed the religious education on his siblings—and the difference between being coerced into watching Disney movies and reading the Bhagavad Gita is purely technical, for wisdom and enlightenment are supposed to come on their own terms and according to the divine schedule. One of the things that comes up in the conversation between Franny and Zooey is that Seymour and Buddy created "freaks" out of their siblings by training them in a boot camp of spirituality.

The question then becomes how to exist in the world of phonies and live in Manhattan performing mundane adult tasks while still seeking enlightenment. The answer is provided in the form of the Fat Lady, as Zooey explains it:

> "I remember about the fifth time I ever went on 'Wise Child.' I subbed for Walt a few times when he was in a cast—remember when he was in that cast? Anyway, I started bitching one night before the broadcast. Seymour'd told me to shine my shoes just as I was going out the door with Waker. I was furious. The studio audience were all morons, the announcer was a moron, the sponsors were morons, and I just damn well wasn't going to shine my shoes for them, I told Seymour. I said they couldn't see them *anyway*, where we sat. He said to shine them anyway. He said to shine them for the Fat Lady. I didn't know what the hell he was talking about, but he had a very Seymour look on his face, and so I did it. He never did tell me who the Fat Lady was, but I shined my shoes for the Fat Lady every time I ever went on the air again."

After Franny confesses that she became mindful of the Fat Lady as well, Zooey makes one of his great pronouncements, as the Salinger italics kick in full force: "But I'll tell you a terrible secret—Are you listening to me? *There isn't anyone out there who isn't Seymour's Fat Lady*."

The Fat Lady becomes a symbol of the trite, unspiritual existence, a world that is ordinary in the worst sense of the word, yet invaluable in its ordinariness. She is the human equivalent of a dead cat's head—someone so worthless in her anonymity, so empty, that she attains a profound meaning in the discourse of Glass spirituality.

I hate to have to say this, after a lifetime of love for Salinger and Franny and Zooey, but this is as phony as it can get: the condescension of the Fat Lady parable; the marked border between "out there," where fat nobodies live in widely spread spiritual darkness, and "in here," the space accessible only if you read your Zen and Bhagavad Gita and other *enlightening* books. But the only difference between "out there" and "in here" is that the people "inside" talk about their pursuit of spirituality, and God knows they talk a lot, while all their practices seem to be as phony as the next person's: Zooey is a phony soap opera actor; Franny is a phony Yale graduate student, and Seymour is the greatest phony of all, with his mishmash of convenient philosophies and his self-congratulating love for Muriel and his freakish spiritual control of his siblings. Yet it is hard not to love them, largely because some phoniness is the inevitable price of adulthood, for an adult has to be mindful of other people and not just pursue his or her heart's spiritual (or corporal for that matter) desires—adulthood may be contaminating, but there are too many contaminated adults, with ulcers and all, to ignore them and treat them as dead cats. The Glass children do what everyone else does all the time—phony things that don't seem to have a clear purpose or a visible reward, going about their quotidian business—but they do it and talk about it as if it were a lifetime of asceticism in a remote monastery.

The inexorable implication of the Fat Lady parable is that spiritual and intellectual superiority, born with personal enlightenment, simply comes from the attitude of the individual, that as long as you are on a spiritual quest, anything you do is all right, and not just all right but spiritual—shining your shoes for the Fat Lady is far more than just shining your shoes. This branding of enlightenment is the first symptom of the omnipresent New Age, self-help idiocy—the Catholicism of the phonies—the belief that any kind of selfishness, self-indulgence, triteness, exploitation, and general ignorance is justifiable, perhaps even desirable, as long as it is a part of some kind of search for enlightenment.[3] The Fat Lady has become the Glass kids' stepmother. Her name is Oprah Winfrey, and they have all become spiritually healthier individuals gobbling up her chicken soup for the soul.

Salinger ends up a long way from wax and olives, embracing spiritual phoniness, celebrating the simple, ubiquitously common process of growing up as a daring spiritual quest: the more daring the quest, the richer you are, the less a part of "out there" you are. Wax and olives and shined shoes thus become a symbol of easily attainable enlightenment, whose only visible consequence is the confidence that you can do nothing spiritu-

---

3. Years ago, in a typical instance of acerbic clear-sightedness, Joan Didion, writing in an essay entitled "Finally (Fashionably) Spurious," about *Franny and Zooey*, asserted that "there is a kind of lulling charm in being assured in that dazzling Salinger prose that one's raw nerves, one's urban hangover, one's very horridness, is really not horridness at all but instead a kind of dark night of the soul; there is something very attractive about being told that one finds en*light*enment or *peace* by something as eminently within the realm of the possible as tolerance toward television writers and section men, that one can find the peace which passeth understanding simply by looking for Christ in one's date for the Yale game . . . *Franny and Zooey* is finally spurious, and what makes it spurious is Salinger's tendency to flatter the essential triviality within each of its readers, his predilection for giving instructions for living. What gives the book its extremely potent appeal is precisely that it is self-help copy; it emerges finally as *Positive Thinking* for the upper classes, as *Double Your Energy and Live Without Fatigue* for Sarah Lawrence girls."

ally wrong, because you can find Jesus or the Buddha anywhere, including the stock market or a soap opera, as long as you search for them or *it*. Wax and olives thus become something else, they attain the spiritual market value, becoming in the process the ultimate commodity—something that would be completely useless if it wasn't for its mystical, spiritual essence, something that you can put a price tag on and order via the Internet.

For Sybil, wax and olives were just things pleasant to touch or chew. But Sybil has grown up, ending her spiritual quest in Florida, while her children are regulars in a Manhattan gym, running on a treadmill like hamsters, in perpetual pursuit of self-empowering fitness, spiritual peace, and personal enlightenment. And every morning they drink a large glass of olive oil, because it is good for them, because it makes them different from people who don't.

The Trouble with Franny

Lucinda Rosenfeld

Of all the leading ladies of American literature who end up supine on sofas, nursing advanced cases of ennui, it is tortured young sophisticate, college sophomore, and former Whiz Kid, Franny Glass, curled up under an afghan in her dippy vaudevillian parents' messy East Side of Manhattan apartment, who made the most vivid impression on me growing up. Even more vivid was she than the image of Daisy Buchanan and Jordan Baker sprawled akimbo on that white sofa in those billowing white dresses, contemplating another scorching August afternoon on Long Island with nothing to do. Not because the former is any more lucidly drawn than the latter, but because I related better to Franny, being the impressionable baby sister in an artsy-fartsy family with a cluttered house and a Jewish last name (as opposed to a High Society flapper and committed member of the idle rich), even while I couldn't *fully* relate to her, not being an exceptionally pretty and intermittently haughty aspiring actress with a cigarette in one hand and a Yale boy in the other. Not to mention the fact that I had never had a nervous breakdown—moreover, found the very idea of crying in front of one's parents vaguely mortifying.

It should be said, however, that back then I found the idea of most things vaguely mortifying. And still, that such a seemingly well-adjusted girl as Franny might be driven to religious fanaticism and mental collapse merely by being alive in the world made perfect sense to me, given (what I felt to be) the general lousiness of people in particular, and the what's-the-point-ness of life in general. It is this arguably infantile and (to a certain kind of teenager) irresistible outlook that made me a prime candidate for a Salinger Phase. And a Salinger Phase I had, albeit briefly, around the age of sixteen, not least because *The Catcher in the Rye*—which tends to jump-start these things—was and is required reading in nearly every high school in America, including my alma mater. And while *Catcher* was and is the story of one boy and therefore, ultimately, a boy's book, fart jokes and all, the uncanny, unflinching realism on display between its covers was enough to propel me into the not-so-warm embrace of *Nine Stories*, and later, *Franny and Zooey*, and *Raise High the Roof Beam, Carpenters*.

Curious to know how *Franny* would hold up after fifteen years away, I reread it earlier this year. In truth, I had forgotten almost everything about the book except that I adored it. I was therefore surprised to discover that the story opens with neither Franny nor Zooey but rather with Franny's full-of-himself boyfriend, Lane, shown here to be re-reading Franny's most recent love letter to him in anticipation of her imminent arrival from a nearby college and just in time to catch the Yale game. My first thought was that there was something incredibly precious about the whole scenario, not to mention the setting. (And did it really have to be named as "the Yale game"—as if that automatically connotes some special kind of meaning?) My second thought was that there was something slightly pathetic about the fact that Salinger, by then in his mid-thirties and onto his third book, was still writing about a bunch of adolescent preppies. My third thought was that I had extrapolated this last idea (of Salinger having a prejudice against adult subjects) from a review I'd read of daughter Margaret Salinger's recently published memoir, *Dream Catcher*, in which the suggestion was made that J.D. only loved her as a child—and, what's more, was somehow uninterested and even repulsed by the foibles of mature love.

All of which raises the question as to what extent the experience of reading Salinger has been tainted by the spate of unflattering portraits of the author that have seen print in recent years—in particular, Joyce Maynard's *At Home in the World*, in which the author recounts her teenage liaison with the Great Man (revealed here to be a urine-drinking sadist). The issue is a tricky one, not least because so many of our best writers seem to have been intolerable and/or intolerant people who went out of their way to make their intimates' lives a misery. Or is it rather that if you scratch the surface of anyone's life (my own included), it will reveal all kinds of unpleasantries that, taken out of context, seem like pure evil, where once and in context they seemed inevitable? My own feelings on the subject of artist versus artistry are all over the map. On the one hand, I continue to believe that the personal is political, and that—especially where the opposite sex is concerned—there is something grotesque about lionizing a pig (to mix a few metaphors), even a talented pig. On the other hand, I hail from a family who, beginning with my grandfather, an abstract painter, has always insisted on the strict division of art and politics. My father, a cellist, is as happy to play Wagner (a famous anti-Semite) as he is Mahler (the only great German Jewish composer), though he probably prefers Mozart (a mere tool of the monarchy!) to them both.

Which perhaps explains why I am somehow able to forgive T. S. Eliot his anti-Semitism. (*The Wasteland* is too beautiful?) Nor do I find myself objecting terribly to those WASP writers who have resorted to unflattering Jewish stereotype (Fitzgerald's Meyer Wolfsheim, for example) to tell their stories. And at the same time I find myself utterly scornful of (to the point of not wanting to read the work of) those Jewish-American male writers whose "big dick" (I can't think how else to say it) complexes have informed their personal lives as well as their professional ones. If I hadn't already been offended by Saul Bellow's famously documented attacks on the women's movement, for example, his need to father a child in his eighties—and with a woman young enough to be his granddaughter—would have pushed me over the edge. I would readily consent that this split in my tolerance gauge simply reflects my being more invested in feminism than I am in Judaism, were it not for the fact that, while I give lip service to my disdain for present-day Woody Allen (who famously ran off with his longtime girlfriend's adopted daughter, Soon-Yi), *Deconstructing Harry*, which postdates Allen's Creep Period by several years, is one of my favorite films of the nineties.

As for J.D., my feelings about the writer versus the writing are complex. For one thing, I am not entirely trustful of Maynard's portrait of him, for the reason that spurned lovers, by nature of being spurned, tend to recall the past in terms of how it seems to justify what later happened. Specifically, their recollections tend to be skewed in the interest of casting themselves as the victims, as opposed to the willing and hungry accomplices they typically were. Maynard's age at the time of the affair complicates matters. But while she famously wore a jumper dress decorated with "ABC's" on her first visit up to the old house in Vermont, she was also a legal adult—it should be noted—as well as a published writer and savvy self-promoter who was certainly aware of her own powers to charm and seduce. Furthermore, on account of Salinger's retreat from society as we know it, we have yet to hear his side of the story, and probably never will. And finally, if the guy wants to drink his own urine, who am I to pass judgment?

In the end, of course, brilliant writing tends to steamroll everything in its path. And there are fleeting moments in *Franny* that achieve exactly this. One example is Franny's arrival in New Haven, which is so delicious in its rendering as to forgive the tongue kiss earlier afforded Lane and his maroon cashmere scarf. (" 'I've missed you.' The words were no sooner out than she realized that she didn't mean them at all. Again with guilt, she took Lane's hand and tight, warmly laced fingers with him," he writes.) What Salinger captures perfectly is the schizophrenia and hyperconsciousness of our youthful love affairs, and how, before we possess the courage of our convictions, the pendulum seems to swing, sometimes midsentence, between repulsion and ardor, suspicion and remorse, loathing and self-loathing, with every gesture examined to the nth de-grec for evidence of The Truth. With Franny, Salinger also taps into the feminine disposition to please at all costs—a disposi-tion that, fifty years later, has waned but not disappeared. Indeed, Franny's sudden and urgent loathing for Lane is ever counterbalanced by her wondering what she's done wrong. Such that her pointed comments and petty barbs are all fol-lowed by spluttering apologies—e.g., "I'm way off. I'll just ruin the whole weekend. Maybe there's a trapdoor under my chair, and I'll just disappear."

Does Fanny have the right to "call" Lane on his intellec-tual pretensions and egomania? Or is she being a rude and un-grateful guest? This is the question that haunts Franny throughout their ill-fated lunch at the Dickensian-named Sickler's, and eventually leads to her bowing out—both liter-ally and figuratively—of the entire problematic. I seem to re-call as a younger reader finding Franny's barside fainting spell sweet revenge, not merely because it leaves Lane dateless for the big game, and at the same time (one presumes) confined to her side as an unwitting nurse, but because it seemed so deeply antithetical to the whole Ivy League spectacle in all its preten-sions to civilized merry-making. Fifteen years later, however, I would have preferred to see Franny tell Lane he was a preten-tious fuck, and walk out! Just as I found Franny's wipeout to be a disappointingly Victorian narrative twist, which has the effect of blotting out much of the excitement one feels for the character in all her fidgety impudence in the previous two scenes. Once a firebrand, in one literal fell swoop, she is ren-dered a victim of her own frailty, and therefore unaccountable for any of the opinions, tart or otherwise, she's previously voiced. I think there's a danger in reading literature solely in terms of politics—gender, racial, or otherwise—and I don't want to do that here. Characters often do the opposite of what we might like them to do; that's no fault of the book. Still, where characters make bad choices, or, in this case, bow out of making any choice at all, the reader (it seems to me) is allowed to be disappointed.

And at the same time—and perhaps this better explains my impatience with the scene's finale—I recognize the impulse (away from accountability, and toward the safe-haven of frailty) as my own. At Franny's approximate fictional age (twenty), I too employed mental and physical weakness as a defense against my own opinions, not because I didn't feel smart or important enough to have any, but because it was *more* important to me to inspire sympathy and protectiveness—I suppose as a deterrent against being abandoned by whoever it was I didn't want to be abandoned by. But even with my age and experience, I am still aware of the fleeting desire to fall sick in the company of men, and not just on account of the attention it's likely to win me, but because illness, its physical discomforts aside, can come as a welcome respite from the problems and seeming impossibility of adult life and love.

I am also guilty—if that is the word—of allowing my fictional characters to seek solace in frailty. In my first novel, *What She Saw . . . ,* my twenty-year-old fictional heroine, Phoebe Fine, engages not just in ego-erasing relationships, but in self-starvation both as a means of self-protection and also of reinventing herself. ("She wanted to be empty—empty so he could overwrite her. So she was not herself—someone else . . . And because she wanted to be so empty that her recent past—

her recent failures and rejections—would become irrelevant. So she could start from scratch—a blank slate, pure unadulterated epithelium, two-dimensional and in no hurry to become three. So all you saw was all you got. So ordinary people couldn't get under your skin . . .") In short, having written a character study of a woman who searches for herself in fifteen different men, it is hard for me to argue that female heroines, in order to be effective characters, need be role models for young women everywhere! Nor can I claim that my character "learns her lesson" in any sense of that phrase. In fact, the last chapter of *What She Saw* . . . finds Phoebe placing her hopes in one more frivolous affair—this time, with a cute actor named Bo Pierce.

Perhaps one would feel more sympathy for Franny if—with the opening of part two and her subsequent retreat to the family afghan—she didn't seem quite so clueless with regard to her own collapse. Unfortunately, between her obsessive supplications to a higher power and her lachrymose cat petting, Franny quickly mutates into a bit player in her brothers' drama. As it later emerges, it is deceased brother Seymour Glass—whose suicide is famously detailed in the first of nine stories, "A Perfect Day for Bananafish"—who has put the idea into Franny's mind that the only path to an honest life involves the tireless recitation of an obscure prayer. Though if the idea for Franny's breakdown can be traced back to Seymour, then the cure belongs to surly actor-brother, Zooey Glass, masquerading as recluse-brother, Buddy Glass. In all fairness, Franny does engage in a few ripe exchanges with Zooey, including a few lurching attempts to take responsibility for her struggles. ("What do you think I'm doing here in this crazy room—losing weight like mad, worrying Bessie and Les absolutely silly, upsetting the house, and everything?") But it is ultimately Zooey who answers that question for Franny. And what a long answer it is! Zooey's expounding on civilization and its discontents goes on and on—and on. One might be forgiven for thinking that Salinger is trying a tad too hard to make a hero out of a chump. Indeed, the tough-love-is-the-right-kind-of-love message comes across loud and clear—it seems to me—without the need for such grandiose lines as, "This is God's universe, buddy, not yours, and he has the final say about what's ego and what isn't." (Did people really ever talk to their brothers and sisters this way?) Conversely, the scorn Salinger reserves for worrywart mom, Bessie Glass—soon retired to the sidelines with her ineffectual and (we're meant to think) laughable efforts to get Franny to consume some chicken soup—seems excessive and (dare I say?) misogynistic. Curiously, there is no sign of or word from father, Les Glass.

In my high school, seniors got to design their own yearbook pages. I can no longer locate mine (no doubt on purpose), but I seem to remember including—or maybe I only thought about including but decided it was too mortifying—the following quotation: "An artist's only concern is to shoot for some kind of perfection, and *on his own terms*, not anyone else's." It is from Zooey's final monologue: the one about shining your shoes for the "Fat Lady," a hypothetical construct meant to signify the universality of God. And it is the only passage in the book that has stuck with me all these years. It's about being true to yourself, and to your vision, even if you're the only one who seems to appreciate it. I still love that line, still believe in the message—even if I'm old enough to realize that it's somewhat adolescent, not to mention untenable in a capitalist society in which lunch must be paid for. Still, there is something to be said for such a brand of self-aggrandizement in the context of fiction writing—a form that, quite literally, requires a total suspension of outside voices (other than those being intuited on the computer, the typewriter, or the yellow pad). Salinger must have known this. If the rebellions in *Franny* fail to pack much of a punch, the prose still, occasionally, and in the context of its own terms, achieves *some kind of perfection*.

Franny and Amy

AMY SOHN

Though pouring down rain, Thursday evening was parka weather, not slicker weather as it had been all week—because at dusk the temperature had dropped to bitter cold, and as the rain fell it turned to sleet. Of the seven wet hipsters waiting on the platform of the Lorimer Street station for the Manhattan-bound train at 9:05 P.M., not more than a few were without woolen hats. Amy, in a long black coat, was one of these people.

She was on her way to a date with a man named Max Blonstein, and wanted very much to appear stylish and to-gether. Because it is impossible for a woman to be both sultry and warm at the same time, Amy had opted for the former over the latter, and chosen the coat, suede, with a filmy red scarf around the neck, in lieu of a hat. She regretted it now as she shivered and waited, but tried to soothe herself by recalling what her mother used to say when she was combing the knots out of young Amy's hair: "It hurts to be beautiful."

After fifteen minutes the train came and Amy piled on with the bespectacled youths. The car was mostly empty—few Brooklynites can muster up the energy to return to Manhattan after nine at night—and Amy was relieved to have an entire row of seats for herself. She tilted her chin up and spent a few minutes perusing the messages against sexually transmitted diseases, and then she pulled a small paperback book out of her handbag.

The cover was white but dirty and peeling free from the spine. The pages were brown with age and some of the edges had already crumbled off. She had gotten the book when she was sixteen, acting in a play. One of the older male actors had befriended her and given it to her as an opening-night present. She had read it over the next few days and been moved to tears by its honesty and heart; the characters were real and brilliant and sensitive, the kind of people teenagers liked to fancy they were, and they had difficulties with the world and its lack of truth.

On this evening, approximately ten years later, she had decided to read it again, not sure why. She had about thirty unread books on her shelf and in general tried not to waste her time with old ones, but that afternoon, feeling morose and empty and Sunday blue, she had gone over to the shelf and selected it on a whim. She had read it in one sitting on the couch and had suddenly felt less morose and more alive. As she was dressing to meet Max, she had spotted it still lying on the couch and instinctively slipped it into her bag.

As the train made its way into Manhattan, she ran her

hand over the cover, removed her bookmark, a stub for a movie she could not remember having seen, and opened it up. The scene was a man greeting his girlfriend, and after a few sentences Amy began to daydream about her upcoming date. It was their second, most crucial one, and she hoped it would go well.

Amy had met Max at a party, through a mutual friend. She had been pleased by his look—medium-sized and medium-attractive, with messy brown hair and brown glasses. As soon as they were introduced, his eyes had bulged out of his head and he had exclaimed, "*Hello*!" She had quickly determined that his energy was at that strange midpoint between childlike and homosexual—he listened as though he was wildly enthusiastic about everything she had to say. But Amy had neither minded nor suspected latency because it had been a long time since she'd met a man who was wildly enthusiastic about anything, much less her.

As they chatted, Max told her he wrote punchlines for a late-night television show. Before he left the party he took her number and gave her one of his business cards. His name was printed in the center, but instead of PUNCHLINE WRITER underneath, it said SHORT ORDER COOK. Amy had laughed aloud at this, and Max had nodded as though proud of his quick wit.

Later that week they made a date to go to the theater to see a period play about a doomed love affair. Eighteen minutes into the play he grabbed her hand and held it on and off until the curtain call. She felt comfortable and easy with him, and flattered that he'd touched her first. Most times she was the aggressor.

After the show, as they walked out of the theater Max said,

"I have to get up early tomorrow but do you want to come over for a little while?"

"Yes, I would," she said, squeezing his arm excitedly.

When they got there she discovered that he owned an upright piano. She had taken lessons as a child but had not played much since, so she sat down and impressed him by playing the themes from *Love Story* and *Terms of Endearment*.

When she finished she moved to the couch. He followed, and high on the play, the piano, and the man, Amy accosted him immediately. He seemed to surrender, but after a few minutes he pulled away to say, "I'm getting really excited but it makes me kind of scared. And I have this work to do and I'm afraid if I get too excited I'll never do it. So I feel like we should stop."

Amy nodded understandingly. She was highly skilled at taking on the expression of a woman who knows how important a man's productivity is to his sense of worth. She was skilled at making this face with men she dated because she had to make it so often, but every time she did she got hit with a spell of loathing for their small-bandwidth brains and their reckless, unapologetic self-importance. This loathing for them was always followed by a longer, much sadder loathing for herself.

She stood up and put on her coat and Max walked her to the front door of his apartment. As she put her hand on the knob he said, "I should walk you downstairs." But he did not move to put on his shoes.

"That's all right," said Amy, meaning it. "You don't have to."

"I promise I'll walk you downstairs the next time," he said

encouragingly. At first she was comforted by this statement (she wanted there to be a next time and now she felt sure there would). Then she thought about it and wondered why, if he really felt in his gut that walking her downstairs was the right thing to do, he didn't just do it *this* time.

The L train arrived at Amy's stop and she closed the book and put it back in her handbag. She walked slowly to the bar, arrived at 9:32, and opted to go inside despite the fact that she was only two minutes late for the date.

The bar was mobbed and throbbing. Loud music was pulsing on the stereo and the televisions showed closed-captioned beer commercials. She did a tour from front to back, scanning the faces for Max, but he wasn't there. She briefly considered leaving and coming back ten minutes later so she would be the second to arrive, but it was still sleeting outside and she didn't have the energy to venture out again solely in the interest of romantic posturing.

She found a seat by the door, near a beautiful, slender brunette who was sitting with a much less attractive, owlish man. Just as she was wondering what his draw was, Max came in, wearing a waistlong puffy parka.

He stopped two feet away from Amy but didn't see her because she was so close. Instead he looked across the room, stuck his chin out, and squinted through his glasses. Amy wondered whether a woman sitting across the room who spotted them together might have wondered what his draw was too.

Amy watched him a few more seconds and then stood, tugged on his sleeve, and said, "Max."

His face lit up. He wrapped his parka'd arms around her,

kissed her on the lips, and said her name. She felt he was over-joyed to see her.

In fact he wasn't completely overjoyed. For the past few weeks Max had been attempting to sell a pilot for a television show about a group of male comedian friends, *Stand Up Guys*. He had gone to Hollywood and had what he thought were several particularly promising meetings, but this morning his agent had called to say two of the networks had passed. The agent had told Max the networks had felt the characters were "a little too cocky and dark to be saleable."

Max had been so dismayed by this conversation that he had been in a miserable mood all day at work, and had even considered calling Amy to cancel. He had decided against it, however, because lately he had been working on not running away from things he wanted.

"I'm sorry I'm late," he said, putting his hand on her arm. "I couldn't get a cab."

"That's all right," she said.

"We're going to have a very good time together."

"I know," said Amy, wondering whether he was trying to convince her or himself.

"It's so loud here," he said. "Let's go somewhere else. There's a restaurant across the street that's quiet and kind of romantic."

He linked his arm through hers and they walked outside. It had grown even colder, and Amy enjoyed being on the arm of a man, even a same-height man, because it made her feel taken care of. She didn't often feel the need to be taken care of, but when she did it was usually at the very beginning of winter

when happy couples seemed to emerge from every corner—
men helping women out of cabs, holding their coats for them
as they left restaurants, lighting their cigarettes under falling
snow.

The restaurant was an old-fashioned tavern not far away.
A waitress, a heavy woman who looked as though she might
have once been a truck driver, led them to a table in the back,
by a group of three women who were clucking at photographs.

"I'm so hungry," said Max as the waitress handed them
the menus. "I barely ate a thing all day. Are *you*?"

"I ate already," she said. "But go ahead. Eat as much as
you want." Max opened the menu and looked at it anxiously.
Amy felt a wave of affection for him as she watched him deliberate. She reached over and squeezed his shoulder, aware that
she was being forward but not wanting it to matter. He put his
hand on her hand for a moment without looking at her, then
took it away and rested it on the menu.

The waitress came, and inquired as to whether they had
made their selections. Amy ordered a glass of white wine.

Max said, "I'm sort of hungry? But not quite hungry
enough to want a huge meal? Can you help me out?"

Amy was charmed by his ability to ask for assistance but
bothered by the way he raised his voice at the end of his sentences. The waitress went down the menu describing the different dishes, their approximate sizes, the way they were
cooked, the accoutrements with which they came, and after a
few minutes of interchange, Max selected the trout.

As soon as the waitress left, Max sighed a little sadly. He
wanted to feel close to Amy, and it suddenly occurred to him
that the best way to do that might be to let her in on his cur-

rent state of mind. He told her about the television pilot and his feelings of frustration.

Amy said, in what she hoped was a comforting tone, "Maybe you'll still sell it."

"That's just the thing, though," said Max. "I'm really not so sure. Good news comes quickly, and it's already been two and a half weeks. I just can't *stand* the idea that all the work I did might be in vain. I've just been paying my dues for so long that I feel like it's about time I got a little artistic validation."

"It must be tough," said Amy.

"I'm sorry if I seem like a drag," said Max.

"I don't think you're a drag."

"I feel like I am," he said. "I definitely don't have my feet on the floor tonight. I've been feeling so good lately, I mean so centered, and settled. Like I'm at a very big transition in my life."

"What kind of transition?"

The waitress set the wine before them and Amy took a large sip.

"For most of the fall I felt so all *over* the place," said Max. "I didn't know what to do with myself, I felt a total inability to just, you know, be present."

"Are you in therapy?" asked Amy.

"Oh yes," said Max. "Since I was eight. I like this new one. I've been seeing her for a year. We've been working really well together. What was I—"

"Being present."

"Right. Lately I've been feeling really lucid, like I'm finally beginning to understand what I want, both as an artist and also out of love. I was seeing a woman over the summer and I knew it wasn't right but I was seeing her anyway because I felt it was time I gave something long-term a chance."

"You can never fake it when it's not right."

"I *know*!" he said. "That's what I finally realized. So it didn't work out, but then when I met you"—Amy's eyes got wide—"you espouse so many of the qualities I'm looking for in a woman and I don't just mean the Jewish thing. I felt so comfortable around you, and you're *smart*, the other woman wasn't smart, and I just, I could finally see it all beginning to happen."

Amy felt as though she had scored a touchdown. She tried to imprint the phrase "I could see it all beginning to happen" on her mind so she could accurately report it to her girlfriends later.

"But today for some reason," said Max, "I feel like I don't know where I am. I don't mean that as an excuse. I hate making excuses for myself because it's not fair. It's not like I'm trying to apologize for how I'm feeling. I'm just trying to explain it."

Amy began to rummage through her handbag for some lipstick. It wasn't that she felt she needed a fresh application, in fact she rarely wore lipstick at all and felt silly applying it in public, but she suddenly needed to do something with her hands.

"The whole reason I'm telling you this," said Max, "is because I don't want you to think this is the norm. 'Cause it isn't." Amy's hand touched something small and phallic. She pulled it out but it turned out to be a double-A battery. She rummaged some more, her fingers moving over a matchbook, a small container of eye shadow, a bottle cap, a pistachio shell, and a lip brush.

"This is a fluky day in an otherwise really good couple of months," said Max. "I just want to eat with you and talk to you and have an excellent time."

Certain she had found the lipstick, Amy removed what turned out to be a small plastic-wrapped feminine item and quickly put it back.

The waitress arrived and put Max's food in front of him. He cut into his trout excitedly.

"So do I," said Amy, beginning to pull the largest items from the bag and set them on the tablecloth.

"What's the book?" said Max.

"*Franny and Zooey*," said Amy, holding it up. "J. D. Salinger."

"I read that in tenth grade."

Amy's heart began to pound in her ear but she made an effort to be casual. "Yeah? What did you think of it?"

"Or maybe it was *Nine Stories*," he said. "I can't really remember. All his stuff blends together. What's it about again?"

"This woman, Franny," she said, watching Max very closely, "goes to visit her boyfriend at college, and basically has a nervous breakdown because she can't deal with how fake the world is."

"Isn't there some whole religious thing in there? She's trying to say the name of God or something?"

"That's right, because she wants to experience—"

"Isn't Salinger a Buddhist?"

"I'm not sure."

"I think he is. Or maybe he's a Siddha Yogi."

"I—"

"Or maybe he's just into yoga."

"I don't think J.D. Salinger does yo—"

"*I* should start doing yoga. I have a really bad lower back and someone told me it's good for that. I used to work out all the time but now I never go. I used to be really pumped. You should have seen me five years ago. But now I'm in lousy shape." Amy smiled at him tightly. "I'm sorry," he said. "Go on."

"Well," said Amy slowly, "I read the book a long time ago too, but today I read it again. I've actually been feeling kind of down the last few weeks."

"Why?"

"I think it's just seasonal affect disorder but this year it hit harder than last. Anyway, when I was done reading the story I just started crying and I wasn't sure why. I really thought Salinger was this author you fall in love with when you're fifteen and think the whole world is phony and then when you read him again you decide he's overrated. But I wound up appreciating him even more."

"You're cute," he said.

"What?"

"You are."

Amy had an image of Max levitating high over the table, and she felt like grabbing his foot to yank him back down.

"Thank you," she said. "I guess what I'm trying to say is that there's something, just, so moving to me about this character who's on this search for some kind of meaning, and she doesn't know how to find it, and she wants to feel it with this man, but—"

Max was waving his hand violently at the waitress, who was standing at the bar. "Is something wrong?" asked Amy.

"I'm sorry," he said. "I bit into something really . . . and this wasn't supposed to have any . . . *Excuse me!*" he called out. "Could I have some water?"

The waitress came over with a glass and set it down on the table. Max chugged it down in a few swift gulps and turned to Amy.

"I was so with you," he said. "Salinger. Story. Search for some kind of meaning." The waitress moved away.

"Yeah," said Amy, gripping the base of her wine glass. "She's visiting her boyfriend for the football game and he has all these great plans for them, but as soon as she gets there he sees something's not quite right. She's starting to lose her shit, basically. She wants to fit inside the box, wear the nice coat, go out with the handsome guy, but a part of her is totally incapable of it. And she realizes that she and this guy, who's supposed to be the love of her life, don't actually have anything in co—"

"That's what I meant about the girl I was seeing this summer! She worked in this juice place I went to. I know it sounds crazy, I dated a juicer, ha ha, you should have heard the jokes my buddies made. But she was really pretty, and so nice, and different from me, and I hadn't been in a relationship for so long."

"It's more than that, though," said Amy. "It's not just that the guy's unsatisfying. It's that everybody she meets is unsatisfying. There's this great line in there where she says, 'I wish I could meet someone I respect' and it's simple, and obvious, and whatever, but I can relate. It's like the process of having to pretend you respect completely idiotic people can become so exhausting that it literally makes it difficult to breathe."

"I know exactly what you mean."

"You do?"

"That's what L.A. is like."

"What are you talking about?"

"That's why no one can breathe there, because the whole city is so phony. I mean there's also one mother of a smog problem, but—" He looked over at her, expecting a smile, but she was looking at him strangely. "That was a joke," he said.

"I got it."

"I'm a comedy writer."

"I know you are."

"I don't think you think I'm funny."

"You have no idea."

"Maybe I'm not funny at all," he said glumly. "Maybe that's why I am utterly incapable of selling my godforsaken show. But I worked so hard on it. And I really had a good feeling and— What's the matter? You don't look so good." Amy's complexion was usually olive but to Max it looked particularly chartreuse now.

"I'm fine," she said. "I think it's just the wine." She raised her hand to her forehead, which was slightly damp.

He put his knife and fork down and pushed the plate away. "So maybe I'll read that book again. You think I should?"

"You might get something out of it," she said, picking up the book and putting it into her bag. "Or maybe you won't."

"No, I feel like I will," he said. "I'm sure it would be particularly good for me to read something depressing at this particularly depressing time in my life. I always think my life would be better if I read but I never do. I'm always saying to myself, 'This month I'm going to read a book,' but I can't get around to it. Sometimes I look at my bookshelf and it's just, so em*barr*assing. It's a bunch of *hu*mor books people give to me because they think, 'Oh, comedian, I bet he wants *hu*mor books.' I have five shelves of bathroom books. In the living room."

Amy regarded him for a second as though trying to remember how she wound up at this particular table with this particular man. Max looked down at his plate forlornly and shoved his glasses up on his nose. Peals of laughter rose from the women at the next table, and then fell.

"Would you excuse me a second?" said Amy.

. . .

THE LAVATORY OF the restaurant was a cramped, unisex, one-toilet room lit by a dim bulb. The tiled floor was filthy and there were a few clumps of toilet paper and paper towels scattered near the waste bin. The faucet of the sink had been left on by the previous occupant and was running lightly. A green bar of soap lay on top of the sink, glistening with bubbles. Amy closed the door behind her, locked it, and leaned against it for a moment.

She went over to the toilet, wiped a few droplets off the seat, and sat down. She breathed in slowly, unzipped the handbag, and took out the book. She looked at the cover, the two green lines running across it about a third of the way down, and ran her finger over them. Then she waited to cry.

She waited a long time. She even scrunched her face up in cry mode because often when she did that tears followed. But nothing came. She was frustrated with her inability to emote; usually she cried too easily too often. She wanted to feel pain but instead she just felt removed, as though she could have seen the whole night coming, as though she was watching the ending of a movie she'd seen before.

She didn't know what was worse, to feel miserable or nothing. In the past, on the other Second-Date Falls, she had gone home and wept at the tragedy of it not working out. Now she just felt tired by the sameness of the stories. She knew part of the problem might be her own tendency to leap, but she didn't want to alter herself because deep down she didn't think the problem was with her. She just wanted one man to be better and different. She wondered when that would happen, and then she realized with a strange sense of calm that she would simply have to wait until it did.

She lifted the book to her face, pressed her cheek against it for a moment, and put it back inside her handbag. Then she stood up, went to the sink, and rinsed her face even though there was nothing to rinse off. She looked at herself in the mirror, blinked a few times, and put her hand on the doorknob.

. . .

WHEN AMY CAME out of the ladies' room she found Max leaning down intently, signing his credit card bill. As she approached he looked up, closed the bill cover, and smiled faintly. She sat down next to him. "Are you OK?" he asked.

"Yeah," she said. "I'm fine."

"You were gone a long time."

"I'm really fine," she said.

"So you're not upset with me."

"No," she said, and she wasn't lying.

He was quiet a moment and then he looked at her a little sadly. "I wanted us to have a good time tonight."

"So you didn't," she said. "Have a good time, I mean."

"Not really, no. Did you have a good time?"

She shook her head from side to side.

He sighed heavily. "I guess part of it's my frame of mind. I don't think I could have a good time with *any*body right now, even the woman of my dreams, but part of it's—"

"Me."

He shrugged sadly. "It's like you said before, you can never fake it when it's not right."

The waitress came, took the bill cover, and told the two of them to have a nice night. "Thanks for dinner," said Amy.

"Don't mention it," said Max.

They made their way through the tables toward the front, and when they got outside it was snowing lightly. Amy and Max said a few things about how they should really keep in touch, and how they both might go to a certain New Year's Eve party on the Lower East Side, but both doubted either was true.

A cab came toward them with a light on in the middle, and Amy, afraid she might lose it to a more opportunistic pedestrian, moved down the sidewalk to hail it. Before she got to the curb, though, Max stepped in front of her and held his arm up to do it himself. The cab stopped and she got inside. She watched the snow fall on his hair, and as he waved, slowly the cab began to move.

The Boy That Had Created
the Disturbance
Reflections on Minor Characters in
Life and *The Catcher in the Rye*

JOHN MCNALLY

The Bread Loaf Writers' Conference is the granddad of writing conferences, initially suggested by Robert Frost and then founded in 1926. The conference is an institution in American letters, an eleven-day orgy of, among other things, poetry and fiction workshops and readings. The readings by both novice and well-known writers are held twice daily inside the Little Theater, a large barn with bleacher seating.

I attended the conference in August of 1999, and on the night that esteemed poet Ed Hirsch was to read, nearly all of the seats in the Little Theater were taken. I was sitting in one of the top bleachers at the far back of the theater with a few of my new friends. Gathered in the row in front of us were the

Bread Loaf fellows—writers fresh with their first published books, a handsome and diverse group of men and women with nothing but the promise of more fortunes ahead of them. In short, the envy of Bread Loaf.

As is the case at most poetry readings, the audience responded to Ed Hirsch's work with soft grunts of affirmation, the usual ooooooohs and ahhhhhs, and the appreciative head bobbing. Then, during a moment of silence, a pregnant pause between stanzas in one of Hirsch's poems, my friend D.G. leaned sideways and let rip the loudest fart I'd ever heard. To give some seismographic sense of its magnitude, I need to take you, dear reader, outside of the Little Theater, where D.G.'s friend Michael was stationed. Michael was smoking a cigarette and waiting for the reading to end. He was several hundred feet away, a wall separated him from us, and yet he clearly heard the resounding blast, too. Not only did he hear it, but he had his suspicions as to where it had originated. For a man *outside* to have heard it, you can only imagine the shock and disgust *inside* the theater. Several dozen people had turned around, hoping to catch the offender. The only person, it seemed, who *didn't* hear it was Ed Hirsch, the poet. Without missing a beat, Hirsch carried on with his poem, reading the next stanza.

I was thirty-three years old that year, my title at the conference was "scholar," and yet I was doing all that I could not to laugh. I stared Zenlike out one of the barn's windows, into the Vermont darkness, emptying my head of all thought; but then I caught D.G.'s reflection in the window, his face contorted from holding back his own laugh, and then I heard him snort, and I couldn't help it: I snorted in return. Lan Samantha Chang—a fiction fellow in the row in front of us—turned around to shoot D.G. a look, but a wave of fumes must have hit her entire row at that exact moment, and all the fellows—soon-to-be Pulitzer Prize–winner Jhumpa Lahiri among them—pitched forward. Poor Lan even gagged.

Months later, D.G. sent an e-mail to me. He signed it, *The Boy That Had Created the Disturbance at the Ed Hirsch reading*.

Edgar Marsalla is "the boy that had created the disturbance" in J.D. Salinger's *The Catcher in the Rye*. Marsalla was sitting in the row in front of Caulfield in the chapel, and during a speech by one of the school's donors, Marsalla "laid this terrific fart" that "damn near blew the roof off." "It was a very crude thing to do, in chapel and all," Caulfield says, "but it was also quite amusing."

But after damn near blowing the roof off with his terrific fart, Edgar Marsalla never returns to *The Catcher in the Rye*. He enters the book, creates a scene, then leaves—the fate of a minor character.

In his book *Aspects of the Novel*, E. M. Forster calls them flat characters. According to Forster, "Flat characters were called 'humours' in the seventeenth century, and are sometimes called types, and sometimes caricatures. In their purest form, they are constructed round a single idea or quality."

Our days and nights are crowded with flat characters—people who, like Edgar Marsalla, enter our lives, make a scene, then leave—but it's the scene they make, large or small, that we remember them by, and by which we define them. (I did not know D.G. before Bread Loaf, and if I had never seen him again afterward, I would always think of him at that Ed Hirsch reading bent over, red-faced and snorting, actually convulsing from trying not to laugh—the perennial grade-school prankster.)

Salinger is a master at the minor (or flat) character, and *The Catcher in the Rye* is full-to-bursting with these folk. There are over fifty-five such characters in the novel—over fifty-five!—many of whom never appear more than once, many of whom, in fact, never actually appear in the book at all, floating ghostlike through the dark recesses of Holden Caulfield's mind. If they *do* appear, they do so as bit players, characters of little or no long-lasting consequence to either Holden or the novel's plot. And yet without these minor or flat characters, *The Catcher in the Rye* would evaporate in our hands. *Poof*: No more book. To excise these characters would be literary genocide, for what we have in *The Catcher in the Rye* is an entire population. My own copy of *The Catcher in the Rye* is a beat-to-hell hardback in its sixty-third printing, an ex–library copy with a protective Mylar cover. Reading the book once again, I placed yellow Post-It notes at the introduction of each minor character, and by the time I finished reading it, the book had become bloated with yellow stickies, names and attributes curling into view. The book had become a tenement, and the characters were peeking out from the pages.

Salinger uses characters the way a pointillist uses paint: stand back and you'll see a portrait of Holden Caulfield. But it's more than that, really, because the *way* that Holden sees these characters says a lot more about Holden Caulfield than it says about any individual character, the cumulative effect of which is that we see, by the end of the novel, not only a portrait of Holden but a blueprint of his psyche as well, his vision of the world.

For my money, this is the beauty of the book. There's much to be said about the *voice* of the novel, but frankly the voice gets a little old in places, and Holden's tics (all of his "and all"s at the end of sentences, or calling everyone "old" so-and-so) start to grate on me, especially once Salinger starts piling them on, sentence after sentence. These tics become a literary affectation, a device to *create* Holden's voice, but devices in and of themselves often call more attention to the creator than the created. The minor characters, however, are gems who don't linger on the scene long enough to grow stale.

There are so damn many characters in *The Catcher in the Rye* that the book becomes a profile of personality prototypes, but what makes the characters unique isn't a set of abstract characteristics. More often than not, Salinger provides us with a gesture, and it's this gesture that pumps blood into the heart of the character, bringing him or her to life. The gesture is so precise, so *perfect*, that we recognize it—we know what sort of person would behave this way—and it becomes difficult to read the novel without matching Salinger's characters to real people we know.

When I read about Ackley, the kid who lives in the room next to Holden's at Pencey, and how when he's done looking at the photo of Sally Hayes, he puts it back in the wrong place, I can't help thinking about this guy I knew in graduate school who was pathological about putting things back in the wrong place, and how it drove me mad. In Barnes and Noble, for instance, he'd take a book off the shelf, and while talking to me, he'd stuff the book back *anywhere* but where it belonged. Whenever I mentioned it to him, he'd get defensive. "Oh, *sorry*," he'd say, and then he'd start huffing and snorting for a while, making a big show of putting everything back in its correct place for the rest of that particular visit. That's Ackley. Holden says, "He did it on purpose. You could tell." You *could* tell. Absolutely. Holden's right.

Even when Holden offers a sweeping generalization about a group of people, the generalization is so fresh and acute that it quickly gloms onto the face of a flesh-and-blood person—one of the many minor characters from our own lives—and then through the act of literary transference, that group takes on a distinct personality and becomes a minor character in its own right, albeit a *cumulative* minor character. Early in the novel Holden says of Pencey, "The more expensive a school is, the more crooks it has—I'm not kidding." The biggest crook I've known was a graduate of one of the most expensive schools in the country, so when Holden makes his proclamation, the Pencey quad, its dormitories, and its classrooms instantly fill up with this mumbling, snickering little shithead whom I knew. Well, actually, he wasn't the *biggest* crook I've known, but he was certainly the most consistent and the most annoying, in large part because he had obviously come from a family with money, and because most of what he did was so petty that you felt guilty calling him on it—or you simply couldn't believe he'd done what he'd done. He'd be standing in front of a parking meter and he'd ask if you had a quarter. When you handed him the quarter, he'd stuff it into his pocket and then start walking away from the meter, striking up a conversation to make you forget that he'd taken your quarter. Or he'd eat with you at a restaurant and then leave just before the waiter delivered the bill. Or he'd try to pay for his beer with the tip you left for the bartender. Or he'd steal books from your house, tucking them inside his coat when you weren't in the same room.

What I'm saying is this: you know these people. Salinger has imbued his novel with enough *types* that surely part of the reason for *The Catcher in the Rye*'s endurance isn't simply what's there on the page but what we, as readers, bring to the page. It's exactly what I tell my students *not* to do when they're talking about one another's stories in class—"Don't critique a story based on your own life experiences or how you, person-ally, could relate to it . . . don't superimpose your own experi-ences onto the story . . . the story must work on its own, with or without your life experiences"—and yet Salinger causes me, to some extent, to reconsider the issue. After all, isn't that part of Salinger's unique genius, his ability to make the reader say, page after page, "Oh, yeah, I relate to Caulfield," or "I know a guy just like Ackley"? Salinger's genius is his ability to create the universal out of the individual. I didn't go to a prep school, after all. I attended piss-poor public schools in the Chicago area's working-class neighborhoods, so on the surface I have nothing in common with Holden and his cast of characters. But it doesn't matter. An Ackley is an Ackley is an Ackley, and I know Salinger's Ackley as well as I know my own Ackley.

Keeping with Forster's theory that flat characters are "cre-ated round a single idea or quality," Salinger uses the single-brushstroke approach to characterization—one sentence, one *swipe* of his brush, and there you have it. We're given a detail or an action or something that the character says, and it's enough to nail the bastard for good. "That's exactly the kind of guy he was," Holden says of Ernest Morrow, who likes to snap his classmates' asses with wet towels, and with each subsequent brushstroke for each new character, the implication is that *this is the sort of person he or she is.*

- The old, bald bellboy with the comb-over.

- Faith Cavendish, former burlesque stripper, who "wasn't exactly a whore or anything but that didn't mind doing it once in a while."

- Sunny, the spooky, skinny prostitute.

- Dick Slagle, who'd say snotty things about Holden's Mark Cross suitcases but then hope that people thought that they were *his* suitcases.

- Louis Shaney, the Catholic kid from Whooton, always looking for an opening to mention the Catholic church in town in order to gauge if Holden was a Catholic, too (Catholics are like that, you know).

- Sally Hayes's mother, who'd do charity work only if "everybody kissed her ass for her when they made a contribution."

- Gertrude Levine, Holden's partner during the museum field trips, whose hands were "always sticky or sweaty or something."

- The woman who cried all through the movie but wouldn't let her own kid go to the bathroom. ("You take somebody that cries their goddam eyes out over phony stuff in the movies, and nine times out of ten they're mean bastards at heart.")

- Holden's "stupid aunt with halitosis," who kept saying "how peaceful" Allie looked in the coffin.

- James Castle, who wouldn't take back what he said about a conceited kid. (Of course, he jumped out of a window and killed himself, but there you have it: bullheadedness at the expense of everything.)

- Richard Kinsella, whose lip quivered when he made a speech.

We do this when we talk about the minor characters in our own lives—it's the shorthand of characterization—but in spontaneous conversation we're more likely to fumble, throwing out too many defining characteristics, waiting for the light to go on in our listener's eyes. *Take my grade-school gym teacher. This was Chicago, the South Side, and he had that surfer look going, you know: blond hair baked to straw from the sun, a big-ass Magnum P.I. mustache, but he was sort of a pedophile, too—always making the seventh-grade girls bend over so that he could stare at their asses . . . You know the type, right?* And if that doesn't nail him down, I might say, *Okay, here's the high-point of this guy's life. He had a tryout for the Rams in the seventies. A tryout, for chrissake. You know the kind of guy I'm talking about, right? A tryout, and he's still talking about it. THAT kind of guy.*

We become Mitchell Sanders in Tim O'Brien's "How to Tell a True War Story": ". . . I could tell how desperately Sanders wanted me to believe him, his frustration at not quite getting the details right, not quite pinning down the final and definitive truth." What we're doing is contradictory, really: we want to nail down the single truth about an individual, and yet we want to capture the universality within that individual that will allow our listener to see both at the same time, the specific person we're talking about as well as the *type* of person. This is the Salinger trick—peering at a character through a microscope with one eye and a telescope with the other eye.

Logic dictates that if our own lives are filled with minor characters, then we must occasionally play the role of minor character in others' lives. And what sort of a minor character are we? What is our single brushstroke? I have to tell you. It's usually not pretty.

Here's a true story. Our family moved around a lot when I was a kid, so I frequently changed schools. In the third grade— my first year in a new grammar school—I had the misfortune of throwing up during class. My stomach took me by surprise, and after I had vomited, I set off a chain reaction among the other weak-stomached students around me. At least three other kids followed suit and vomited, too. A year later, my parents and I moved again—it had nothing to do with me puking—and I attended yet another grade school. Several more years passed, though, before I rejoined my former third-grade classmates in high school, and one guy from that class came up to me in the cafeteria and said, "Hey, I remember you. You're the kid who threw up so much that it covered his entire desk."

Jesus! I thought. *Is this how everyone remembers me? The Kid Who Vomited So Much It Covered His Entire Desk? Will this be my lasting legacy?*

This kid who came up to me in the cafeteria, he didn't seem to remember anything else about me except that I was new to that school, that I had voluminously blown chunks, and that I moved shortly thereafter. No doubt he had worked out his own chain of logic and believed that my leaving the school had to do with my embarrassment at puking, and I have no doubt that after I had moved away he told his theory to anyone who would listen, creating the myth of The Boy Who Vomited So Much It Covered His Entire Desk. Like Holden, this kid was creating his own vision of the world by choosing what (and what *not*) to remember, and his memories, in this instance, certainly said more about him than they did about me. Of course, I didn't realize any of this at the time, and I doubt it would have helped me if I did. Here's where real life and fiction part ways. In real life, we are the protagonist of our own ever-unfolding story, and we must suffer the consequences of how people remember us. In fiction, we play the role of implied friend to the protagonist, and if I were to write a story titled "The Boy Who Vomited So Much It Covered His Entire Desk," I wouldn't write it from my point-of-view. No, I'd choose the other kid— a natural protagonist—because he's the one who, if I were the reader, I'd prefer to pal around with. He's the one telling stories, after all. He's the one painting a distinct view of the world (*his* view), and my role in the story was that of the flat character, a minor character in *his* life.

Maybe this is why I don't write heavily autobiographical short stories. Maybe I'm too passive to play the lead. It's true, though, that when I write stories, the character with whom I most relate, nine times out of ten, is the narrator, particularly if my narrator is younger than I happen to be. I relate to them because I hand over to them my best characteristics. *Here, try this on for size.* Or perhaps what I'm doing is giving them characteristics I *wish* I possessed. As a result, they are more charming than me, more lively, and often funnier. They are like me but not me. They are who I'd *like* to have been, I suppose. The minor characters in my stories are often the heavies. They, too, can be funny, but frequently they are pathetic or sinister or, well, downright creepy. They are, by and large, a sad lot. They're *not* me. Let me repeat: They are not me.

Or are they?

The fact is, we don't like being minor characters. Rarely when we read do we see ourselves as the minor characters. Everyone relates to Holden Caulfield, but no one says, "Hey, I'm that bald guy with the comb-over!" Or, "Hey, I'm that guy who likes to snap people's asses with towels!" Is it that the real-life people who represent these minor characters don't read and so are never privy to seeing themselves in print? Or is it that they *do* read but see only their heroic side? We're all, each of us, the protagonist, right? We're all David Copperfield, Holden Caulfield, Harry Potter. Or is that when we run across ourselves as flat characters, we *do* recognize ourselves but hope that no one else will? "Okay, sure, I'm the guy who liked to snap people's asses, but surely no one will see *me* in *him*." Are some people inherently inclined to be minor characters in life? Or is it just a matter of point-of-view: we see the guy with the comb-over and we think, *Ah, the sad-sack . . . the poor bastard*, but in truth the guy with the comb-over has his own triumphs and failures, however large or small, and he is, in fact, no less a minor character than Holden Caulfield, who, after all, is a failure of sorts too, and could easily become a minor character from, say, Ackley's point of view?

And what of Salinger himself? He's been called a great—if not the greatest—minor writer of the twentieth century. He has, by virtue of his meager output, relegated himself to literature's minor leagues. But there is that other issue, too, the issue of his privacy, his exile. Writing output aside, Salinger has chosen a path that easily lends itself to pigeonholing by the media (*those phonies!*) and by all those people who devour what the media spits out about him. In other words, he has made it easy for people to paint him with a single brushstroke, for people to shrink him to a single word, a single characteristic. Mention Salinger's name to someone who's never read him, who's never been charmed by Holden's voice, who's never met those fifty-plus characters in *The Catcher in the Rye* or any other character in *any* of his books—mention his name, and what are you likely to hear?

Oh, yes, him: the recluse.

Normal People

KAREN E. BENDER

I. Great Books

On one of my first days of eleventh grade at Palisades High School, my English teacher, Mrs. Lewis,* handed out her list of Great Books. This list included such books as *The Stranger*, *Lord of the Flies*, *The Great Gatsby*, *Madame Bovary*, and *Crime and Punishment*. These were the books we were supposed to read before college, that would make us educated, that would prepare us for our lives. They were organized under categories that I presumed were distributed to high school English students all over the country. One was "The Evil in Man's Heart." Another was "Man's Inhumanity to Man." Another was "An Individual's Alienation from Society."

Before this class, I hadn't known that books were organized under such categories. I wanted to be a writer and I

_____

*Not her real name.

117

longed to write a book that would appear on such a list. If I were to reach that point, I believed, I would have become an educated, sophisticated person; I would also have arrived at true literary greatness.

Mrs. Lewis asked us to write a long term paper in which we compared three books from these lists. We would have just a couple weeks to read these books and write these papers; they were supposed to be thirty pages long. Presumably, this was what college was going to be like. My topic was "Pressure of Maturation and Achievement." I was supposed to read the books *The Catcher in the Rye* by J.D. Salinger, and *Beneath the Wheel* and *Demian* by Hermann Hesse.

I was somewhat wary about what was sweetly called "Adult Literature"—for we had begun to read novels in a new and disturbing way. Apparently, writers did not simply write books—they dealt with Themes. When we read *The Lord of the Flies*, Mrs. Lewis stood at her lectern and announced, "In *The Lord of the Flies*, Golding demonstrates The Evil in Man's Heart through superficiality, materialistic concerns, emphasis on conformity, cruelty to the outsider, ostracism, and hostility toward the intellectual." She held up her book. It was full of scribbles, underlined sentences—all of this not done subtly, but with a shrieking red pen. The teacher's underlining was apparently not considered defacement, but rigorous intellectual activity. "This is evidence," she said. "Your papers should contain evidence of the author's arguments."

I wanted to get into a good college; I wanted to learn how to think like an adult. Certainly, when students talked about the emphasis on conformity demonstrating The Evil in Man's Heart, it sounded somewhat smart. Or different, anyway. But sitting at the kitchen table, underlining paragraphs and me-chanically writing CONFORMITY! in the margin, depressed me. This was certainly not how I had read *Charlie and the Chocolate Factory*.

Before this, when I fell in love with a book—*Charlie and the Chocolate Factory, From the Mixed-Up Files of Mrs. Basil E. Frankweiler, The Hobbit*—the book and I became involved in an obsessive relationship. I fiercely read it over and over, try-ing to find sentences or scenes that I might have skipped the first time. I imagined bringing the characters into my family's household, and what we would talk about when we brushed our teeth. The actual people living in our house seemed a little unreal, shadowy. During our relationship, the book was not merely a book—it became part of me.

When I told adults that I was about to read *Catcher*, they got odd and misty-eyed; "You'll *love* it," they said, as though eager to bring me into a strange new club. It was not clear to me what I would gain from joining such a club, for its mem-bers seemed to live in the shadowy, tropical world of adult-hood; I was a little wary. The cover of my parents' old copy from the 1960s featured a picture of Holden wearing a base-ball cap and the authoritative advertising copy: "After you read this book, YOU WILL NEVER FORGET IT." I wanted *Catcher* to be good, and needed it to be good. I was fifteen years old, lonely, and desperate for a book to speak to me, for a book to become part of me the way others had. I wanted pri-vacy when I started the book. Staking out the large, empty room denoted our "family room," I closed the folding doors securely, as though I was about to meet a lover. We lived in a California ranch–style house, and the big glass windows overlooked the backyard. Spotlights burned white circles into the grass, roses stood grandly in the light like movie stars. I stretched out on the couch and began to read.

"If you really want to hear about it, the first thing you'll probably want to know . . ." I did not know if I really liked Holden. He talked about Selma Thurmer and how she had "a big nose and her nails were all bitten down and bleedy-looking and she had these damn falsies that point all over the place." What would he say about me?

But I kept reading. I read it deeply, all the way through, in a few hours. My eyes burned but I kept reading. My mouth got dry. My breath was sticky, thick. I read about Holden's ill-fated meeting with Mr. Spencer and the fight with Stradlater and Holden's exit from Pencey Prep. I read about how he checked into the hotel and how he looked out the window at the hotel. "You'd be surprised what was going on on the other side of the hotel. They didn't even bother to pull their shades down . . . The hotel was lousy with perverts." I kept reading, for I understood something deep about Holden. He did not want to grow up; other people often seemed like aliens; he often felt more comfortable with children than he did with adults. He had run away from school, something I had wanted to do on occasion—I thought he was immensely brave. And he thought he was going crazy. This I loved most of all. I loved him when he believed he was going to disappear after he stepped off the end of a curb; "I had this feeling I'd never get to the other side of the street. I thought I'd just go down, down, down, and nobody'd ever see me again." I had spent my junior high school afternoons seeing a psychoanalyst in Westwood, slowly pacing around the 7-Eleven at the corner because I was always embarrassingly early for my appointment, I clutched a granola bar, because my mother had told me to get a healthy snack, and watched the cars rush down Westwood Boulevard, carrying all the normal people to the rest of their lives. I certainly felt like a crazy person then. Holden was the first person, living or fictional, who admitted his craziness to me.

I cried when I finished the book. I had entered the book and then been hurled back into my world again.

I lay on the couch for some time, looking at the ceiling. In the backyard, the rosebushes looked different, lifting clawed arms to the sky. The dark yard appeared full and brimming, as though new, perplexing things were about to start jumping out from behind the trees.

I went into the den where my family was watching TV.

"Karen's crying!" said one of my sisters.

My parents looked at me.

"What happened?"

"Let me give you a hug."

"Why are you crying, sweetie?"

I looked at them, my family, innocently watching *Dallas*, and I understood something terrible; they did not know me and I did not know them.

"It was good," I said, idiotically.

"*Catcher in the Rye* made Karen cry!" I saw that this would be reduced to a touching family anecdote, which suddenly seemed awful. I had been with Holden, and now I was alone. I felt a hopeless, overwhelming love for him. I wanted so to be with him, to be understood.

· · ·

HOLDEN STARTED MAKING appearances in my high school diaries. After a lengthy discussion of my SAT scores came this:

> I read *Catcher in the Rye*. I cried. I have NEVER cried after reading a book. I don't know—Salinger's low key writing style, Holden Caulfield's disdain for phonies, and just the feeling that the book was written for me just touched me. It got me thinking, though—there have really been no good classics about a girl growing up (except for *Little Women,* which is about 100 years outdated) or on the same level as *Catcher*, *A Separate Peace*, or *Demian*.

There were still a lot of books I hadn't read then, including *Jane Eyre*.

Then, a year later:

> I think the greatest accomplishment for a writer is writing a book (like *Catcher*) where the reader feels, "I'm not alone. Other people feel the same way that I do."

This noble idea was followed by the somewhat bitter comment:

> I mean, how can Faulkner make anyone truly content (or even miserable) after reading his works, when the reader is often too confused to get the point?

I always wanted to know what it was to be another person. I would walk down the street and wonder, What are these people thinking? Are they the same thoughts that I have? What is their happiness like? Their sadness?

Holden let me into his thoughts and feelings in a way no other character had. This became an essential goal for me as a writer—to write things that were honest, that would help people feel that they were not alone.

II. Becoming a Writer

Another diary entry. This time it was freshman year, UC Berkeley:

> Every writing I do now is a commitment. A commitment now that I've legitimized myself, announced my candidacy as a "writer"—now I'm open for suggestions and now I can be rated. Now comes the austere, humorless apprenticeship, the dogged faith in my talent, fledgling that it may be— the search for voices that I admire—the constant, endless quest for the diamond in the shit. Why so much shit? Why can't the subconscious be a little less obstinate?

I was going to become a writer. It was time to become Official. I told myself I was a writer repeatedly, trying to convince myself; it was like telling myself I was a rooster or ant. I did not know how anyone became this wondrous species, and I did not know exactly what I wanted to write; however, it is clear from my diaries that I wanted—quickly—to be published.

Over and over in my diaries, I said I wanted to write the female version of *The Catcher in the Rye*. Or, more specifically, I wanted to write the Jewish-California-female version of *The Catcher in the Rye*. This seemed, at the time, to be an important and necessary contribution to American letters. But looking back, this desire actually seems like one of the first thoughts I had that did mark me as a writer—for writers are compelled by the desire to respond to what they have read, to answer a book in their own way. I loved Holden. That was true. But I was growing dissatisfied, too. There was this business of the girls. There was old Selma Thurmer, and the witches in the bar, the blonde and the two ugly ones, etc. I began to wonder—what would Holden think of me, anyway? Would a female Holden be friends with me? Would she be catty? Pitying? Nice? How would she view the men around her? I wanted to hear her, learn how she would view the world.

So I wanted to respond to Salinger—in my ever-expansive frame of mind, I also wanted to improve upon him. How would I start? I began by copying him, as did many of my classmates. A typical college workshop included a few Salinger clones and a couple of souls writing earnest, convoluted versions of nineteenth-century prose. The Salinger clones were unmistakable—they involved depressed first-person adolescent narrators and ungrammatical sentences. Saying you were a Salinger fan seemed a handy way to avoid learning grammar. I imitated Salinger mercilessly for a couple workshops. How else was I to become a writer? He had to be doing something right to make me love him so. Others (particularly the other Salinger clones, who were understandably wary of each other) were onto me. They criticized me harshly ("Did you just lift this directly from page eighty-two?"). I began to read some other books.

III. Dissecting Holden

When I started at the Iowa Writers' Workshop in 1989, I was a more mature apprentice writer. I had gone through post-*Catcher* phases of wanting to write the Jewish Southern California version of *Lolita*, *Wise Blood*, *Crime and Punishment*, etc. Now, however, coming to the Workshop, I began to want to create my own story and to sound more like myself.

The other students in the workshop made authoritative pronouncements about writing that sounded impressive if not terribly clear. Now students talked of "narrative intent" and the "author/reader barrier" and "the Text." One student, who went on to become a very successful novelist, sat in the student lounge one day and said, "In workshop, they said my story had great authority in the spaces between the words. What am I supposed to do, turn in a blank page?"

Now I read all writers, including Salinger, with the calm, cool eye of a surgeon. As part of my MFA thesis paper, I decided to dissect Holden. What were the components of his voice? How did his style affect the reader? I came up with the astute thesis:

> Holden Caulfield's voice will endure in American literature because his voice could not belong to anyone else. Salinger gives him casual, distinctive

speech patterns, strong opinions about everything, and a tough, wistful sense of humor. We believe from the way Holden's voice rambles, skipping casually from topic to topic, that he is really speaking. His voice has a distinctive rhythm. The details are specific and his.

I felt odd dissecting Holden, as it seemed precisely the sort of activity that he would make fun of.

As part of my MFA thesis, I examined first-person voice and took the first few paragraphs from *Catcher* as an example. I stared at these sentences, I tried to take apart Salinger's prose—but I was not a literary critic; I knew mostly how the words, the sentences, made me *feel*. I was beginning to understand how sentence structure and word choice and diction created certain effects, how to use sensory detail, dialogue, plot. At this point, *Catcher* became less important to me than *Nine Stories*. In these stories, I saw how characters disappeared into their gestures, dialogue, and how Salinger's breath was transformed into perception, scene, craft.

The Workshop divided itself into definite camps regarding Salinger. Some thought "A Perfect Day for Bananafish" was profound; others thought it was silly. Some felt Holden was an intolerable narcissist. Others alleged Salinger's misogyny. There was something thrilling about finding faults with great writers, about laughing at them while drinking bourbon in a dark bar. It was like complaining about a parent. Better yet, the great writers themselves could not answer as we said things like, "Hemingway was the Bret Easton Ellis of the 1920s." Now I can see how we were all going through a sort of writer's adolescence—we had to declare our tastes loudly, savagely, for to actually think about becoming writers was a terrifying proposition. How would we fit into this parade of writers? Was one way to write better or more profound than another?

I listened to the students who were cranky about Salinger, and decided, in a rash moment, to agree with them. It was strangely thrilling—it was like permission to think new thoughts. What other writers could I love, and what new sentences would I be able to write? I went through a period of dissing Salinger, preferring instead Isaac Babel.

IV. My First Novel

After finishing some short stories, a novella beginning, and sundry scraps of one thing or another, I was finally ready to start my first novel. I had many other favorite writers when I began my novel. I adored Carson McCullers. I developed a theory that Salinger had also read and admired her. I saw a similar love of strangeness in their work, a tenderness toward the outsider. I loved Eudora Welty, Grace Paley, Philip Roth, Colette, Flannery O'Connor, John Cheever, and on and on.

When I started my first novel, *Like Normal People*, I wanted to write about growing up. It had been a slow process for me, separating from my family. I was twenty-eight and single when I began my novel, and did not know how to move on to the next stage. How did anyone know how to become a married person? How did anyone know how to become a parent and raise a child?

I wanted my novel to teach me how to grow up. Through my writing process, I had made a new discovery. I had always wanted to know what it would be like to be another person, and now I found that I could write from the point of view of someone else. This seemed wonderfully freeing, and I decided to use fiction to try to transform myself.

So, the hub of my novel is Lena Rose, a forty-five-year-old woman who is slightly mentally retarded, and has the fierce desire to get married and live on her own. The novel is told from two perspectives. One belongs to Lena's mother, Ella, who has the job of trying to help her daughter lead as "normal" a life as possible. The other perspective belongs to Lena's niece, Shelley, a troubled twelve-year-old, who views her junior high school classmates' maturation as a mystery, and who feels as though she "had stopped."

It was a terrific challenge to imagine Ella's experiences as a woman in her forties, fifties, sixties, a wife and mother. Writing Ella forced me both to dig deeply into myself and to imagine I was another person, to try to know things I did not think I knew. But Shelley was, ironically, the character who gave me the most trouble in my novel. I had already been a twelve-year-old girl, and as I wrote Shelley, I kept bumping up against my old self. For a few drafts, she was resourceful or perky; I wanted her to be the confident, able girl I wished I had been. There were points when I considered (and others suggested) cutting her from the novel, focusing on the characters who were stronger—but I believed that she was important; cutting her would have been like killing a part of myself. I needed Shelley to stay in the novel partly because I knew I needed her to try to answer Holden—to express some of the feelings I had had as an adolescent, reading in that empty room at the back of the house.

I wanted to write a character who would speak for that girl—a girl who thought she was insane, who wanted so much to connect to someone, but who wandered the world alone. And these longings led me to this passage in *Like Normal People*, one of the passages I most enjoyed writing:

> She had her own ideas about what would happen when she kissed a boy. She could imagine the strange pressure of his lips on hers, and she hoped that, as their lips touched, his thoughts would come pouring into her head. His thoughts and feelings would pour into her head, as hers would into his, and they would both be so full of their own brilliance that they would not care about anything else at all. She had never asked anyone about this theory, because she secretly hoped she was a genius and had figured it out all by herself. What would it be like to be loved in this way? Did she deserve it? What would she become?

In a way, I was describing reading *Catcher* for the first time when I wrote about such a kiss—for that was my first experience of reading a book in which another person's thoughts and feelings were so wonderfully similar to mine. In *Like Normal People*, I tried to write something that would have comforted me, a young girl in Southern California who thought she was crazy. Salinger made me understand that I wanted to speak, and that I had something to say of my own.

The Salinger Weather

THOMAS BELLER

I was standing on the subway the other day, reading *Raise High the Roof Beam, Carpenters*, by J.D. Salinger, when I looked up and saw a familiar shade of red: the blood red (with yellow letters) of the cover of *The Catcher in the Rye*, which is what the book used to look like before the publishing house Little, Brown decided to release all of Salinger's books in these uniform paper white editions with little rainbow stripes in the corners.[1] The young man reading

---

1. Little, Brown issued a new trade paperback last month with the original artwork. They wouldn't say whether the author had weighed in on the matter, but a friend's wife's father (how's that for a reliable source!) who used to work at Little, Brown back when they were publishing his hardbacks, says that when they published *Franny and Zooey* they used black letters on a white background, and the white, the exact nature of the white, was a source of serious discussion and contention between author and publisher. Salinger insisted on just the *right* white, and the company express-mailed him numerous different variations of the color until he finally mailed them back his preference in the form of a small paint chip.

it had a beard and long brown hair pulled tightly behind his head in some kind of mysterious ponytail that hid the tail.

I made my way toward him. I was going to have a random city bonding moment with this guy and find out what was going on with him and J.D. Salinger. It wasn't hard to stop my own reading, because I was on page three, having just finished the long quotation of a Taoist tale ("Duke Mu of Chin said to Lo Po: 'You are now advanced in years,' " it begins) that Seymour Glass reads to his crying, ten-month-old sister Franny in order to calm her. I had been checking the copyright page to see if there was some kind of credit for this tale, or if Salinger had invented Duke Mu and Lo Po (there was no credit, but perhaps you don't have to credit ancient Taoist tales on the copyright page).

You see, I wasn't really reading *Raise High the Roof Beam, Carpenters*. I was staring at it, or past it, in the same way that, for weeks now, I have only been able to *peer* at Salinger, as though the pages themselves were producing a glare.

Was I bored with him? Too familiar? Did the whole spirit of reading him in order to write about him evoke some long-ago homework assignment? I think it's that I was reading him in order to make sense of him, and one of the beautiful things about Salinger's writing is the way it sort of bypasses the realm of logic. Capricious emotions, unlikely circumstances, the power of a whim all reign supreme in Salinger World—and here I was going to try and make sense of it all. Salinger—the man, as opposed to the writer—has such an aura of paranoia about him at this point that to try and put anything interpretive down on the page feels like an attack. And I don't want to attack. But neither do I want this essay to be a bumper sticker saying, I LOVE JD SALINGER!

With such a conundrum buzzing around and interrupting my reading, I was glad for the chance to communicate with a complete stranger. He was sitting, knees close together, and I loomed before him, trying to figure out how to begin.

"Excuse me," I said.

His eyes raised up from his book. I smiled and held out my white copy of *Carpenters* as though it were a badge.

"No thank you," he mumbled, and lowered his eyes again to the page.

"Excuse me," I said again and pushed the book forward more emphatically. "I was just standing over there reading J.D. Salinger and I looked up and saw you were reading him too, and I thought it was weird and wanted to come over and see what you were making of him, if you'd read him before . . ." I went on like this for a bit longer until the extremely thick don't-bother-to-solicit-me-sing-to-me-or-preach-to-me membrane (made extra thick that day by the fact that it was cold and rainy and everyone was swaddled up and trying not to pay attention to the unpleasant dirt-collecting moisture all around them) had been burned through.

He looked up at last and said, "I'm reading it because of my girlfriend." He went on to explain, in tones that were a bit too clipped and careful and, well, scientific for my taste, by which I mean he spoke with a certain measured roboticism, that he had been an engineering major in college and therefore had missed out on "the liberal arts," having read mostly science fiction books outside of his schoolwork, but he was now trying to rectify that by reading all of these books that his girlfriend, who presumably did have a liberal arts education, gave him to read.

"Actually," he said, "she gets these books from her mother. So this is actually her mother's copy."

I forgot to ask if there was some kind of trade-off here between boyfriend and girlfriend—if the girlfriend was getting assignments to go visit slashdot.org or read *Fast Company* and *Wired* or watch sports or listen to Phish, or if the fact that she was getting books from her mother meant that the girlfriend was undergoing her own remedial tutorial from her mother in the Great Books of Mom's Youth, or if the mother, sensing certain deficiencies in the sensuous/intuitive/humanoid/liberal artsy skills of her daughter's boyfriend (deficiencies that were conveyed tearfully during a mother-daughter heart-to-heart?), had suggested her daughter put the engineering/robot-loving boyfriend on a crash course of soul-awakening books—and instead asked what he thought of *The Catcher in the Rye*.

He wrinkled his nose and made a face. "Kind of annoying, actually," he said.

I admired him for this opinion and at the same time wrote him off as a fool.

"Is it the voice? All those old-fashioned slang expressions?" I asked.

"It's just kind of whiny," he said.

"Yeah, I know what you mean," I said and grinned idiotically, as though that was exactly how I felt.

At this point the train pulled into Times Square. It was his stop, and he neatly inserted a bookmark into the book's brittle, yellowed pages. He seemed to be about thirty pages in. Something about this gesture made me feel sure he would finish the book, however annoying he found it.

We said good-bye. Well, I thought, he doesn't get it; his loss (to hell with him!).

The truth is I'm always a little happy to encounter hostility to Salinger; it makes it easier to be his unabashed advocate, it helps remind me of the things I love about him. The way he picks certain spots in which to slow the action to real time, for example, which is part of his magical realism. Salinger's magical realism is not to be confused with the Gabriel García Márquez School of fantasticalness; rather, Salinger renders things, people, situations, and dialogue with such realistic precision that reality becomes imbued with a kind of magic, a kind of hyperclarity.

Alone with J.D., on the other hand, I sometimes get a little jumpy. I was alone with him now, the book in my hand, and I couldn't even read more than a few pages at a time, so who was I to wave the Salinger flag? Something was holding me back from accessing the incredible pleasure I had once felt upon encountering his sensibility. What was it?

. . .

J.D. SALINGER'S WRITING is like a certain kind of weather. It's an atmosphere which, once encountered, permeates everything else. It's a kind of Shangri-La, a paradise where the emotions are acute, the tone is sharp, wisecracky, irreverent, and real, and the phonies are, if not exactly vanquished, then put in their place, identified, and properly insulted (not that they care; they're phonies, after all).

And what exactly is the Salinger Weather like? Is it sunny, cloudy, pouring rain? Is it as suffocatingly hot as the day in which *Carpenters* takes place, or as cold as the day Holden wonders about the ducks in *The Catcher in the Rye*?

The Salinger Weather is one in which there is a coat. You are either wearing it, or carrying it, or wishing you hadn't brought it, or wondering if you should have, or dimly remembering what it's like to be in weather that requires one. The Salinger Weather requires pockets, secrets, privacy, a place where your hands can hide, touching a letter or some bit of memorabilia, a photo, the "If found, please return to . . ." ID card of someone who is no longer living, things like that.

I had a friend whose life took place in the Salinger Weather. He walked around with the weather system hanging over his head in the manner of one of those characters from Charlie Brown (was it Charlie himself?) who walks down the street with a tiny rain cloud directly over his head. Not that the weather is dreary or heavy. It can be sunny and upbeat. The thing is, it's private, it's deeply personal.

The friend's name was Anderson. It was because of Anderson that, in my early twenties, I went back and reread[2] Salinger.

Anderson was a guy with a lot of pockets. He held things

---

2. Like a lot of people, I had *The Catcher in the Rye* as homework, and my initial experience of the book was colored by a pretty intense eighth-grade teacher. Mr. Colan was responsible for introducing me to *The Catcher in the Rye*, which belongs to a generally unremarked-upon literary pantheon: the eight-grade canon. Other members of the canon are *A Separate Peace* and *To Kill a Mockingbird*. Mr. Colan jazzed his up with *On the Road*. Then there is the extracurricular canon, even more flexible. In my case, highlights included *Dinky Hocker Shoots Smack*, *Forever*, and *The Basketball Diaries*.

Mr. Colan was a powerfully built man in his mid to late twenties who could be seen in the hallway on his way to class in a flannel shirt with the sleeves rolled up, one hand holding a stack of books, the other holding a steaming cup of coffee out in front of him at around chest level; sometimes he would crouch over the cup as he walked and take a sip. Some people have a high center of gravity, some people have a low center of gravity. Mr. Colan's center of gravity was this cup of coffee. It was the center of his universe. I mention this because, in hindsight, it seems likely Mr. Colan was living in the Salinger Weather as well.

closely. These things included people he loved, and *things* he loved. In his possession, certain objects became talismans: old books, letters, shirts. Personally, I have a thing for T-shirts, they're really evocative artifacts; even a really mundane T-shirt that you are sure you will never wear will become, if you keep it long enough, a kind of souvenir from a long past chapter of your life. Anderson's relationship to T-shirts, however, was Byzantine, almost erotic; certain of them were sacred objects, and he would not let them go. Several shirts were kept in active duty well past the point where any rational person would have discarded them as rags. He wore them over other shirts for the sake of decency; at a certain point he simply kept them, ghostly remnants of what they once were, evidence of who he once was when he first wore them, when both the shirt and the man were newer to the world.

Anderson's connoisseurship extended to vegetables (in any pile of tomatoes there is one blessed tomato, and to settle for anything less was to deprive yourself of the depth of tomato-ness that is part of life's bounty), sports teams (deep, abiding loyalties), and, perhaps most of all, colors. Certain colors were of enormous value. A certain shade of orange would send him into a faraway place. I won't even attempt to describe how it worked with women.

With writers he was the same way. His voice was whispery, and often became more so when he was enthusiastic. On Salinger he was barely audible. He didn't like loudness, but rather *fine-ness*. At a certain point the love became inarticulable; it existed in an octave the normal ear is incapable of hearing.

All of this I found extremely attractive, *wise*, even, a way to live that made living more worthwhile, and after we had talked a fair bit about writing, I started to realize that a lot of Anderson's sensibility came from J.D. Salinger.

Now, the process of how a writer influences a person is sort of circular. People don't get instructions about how to live from writers, exactly, but sometimes there is something about a writer's voice and worldview that has a clarifying effect on your own self-perception. Writers are particularly susceptible to the Salinger Weather because it is thrilling to see, in Salinger's example, how a writer's sensibility and tone can have such power to shape the way one feels about the world.

Did Anderson get formed by Salinger? No, I don't think so. I don't think people change themselves to match the heroes they meet in books, or the writers who dreamed them up. But a certain voice can make a reader visible to themselves in a way they weren't before. That, at least, is how *I* responded to Salinger. When I read him, post-Anderson, I thought, Yes! So much of what I'm interested in was right there on the page. As writers, we shared values, Salinger and I. By values I mean the way Salinger takes little things—objects, bits of dialog that seem trivial, letters, small moments—and imbues them with importance, allows them to assume, at certain times, a great deal of weight. And also the way he takes big things—a death in the family, for example—and grants them the status of landmarks without being overly sentimental (though he is not perfect, and he does at times swerve pretty close to the sentimental curb, particularly in the later work, such as *Carpenters* and *Seymour*).

A little on magical realism:

In *Carpenters*, a huge part of the story takes place in the backseat of a cab. It's almost exhausting how much time we spend stuck in the sweltering cab along with the overbearing matron of honor, bitching relentlessly about Seymour's unexplained absence from his own wedding; Buddy's only conceivable ally is a "tiny elderly man in a top hat and cutaway, who was holding an unlit clear-Havana[3] cigar." The cab is stuck in traffic, and so, in a way, is the whole story. We're trapped, along with Buddy, in a suffocating cab, with no hope for release. Then the following situation arises:

> "Let's see if we can get a little action around here," the matron of honor's husband said. It was rather the voice of a man who keeps calm under fire. I felt him deploying behind me, and then, abruptly, his head craned into the limited space between Mrs. Silsburn and me. "Driver," he said peremptorily, and waited for a response. When it came with promptness, his voice became a bit more tactile, democratic: "How long do you think we'll be tied up here?"

> The driver turned around. "You got me, Mac," he said. He faced front again. He was absorbed in what was going on at the intersection. A minute earlier, a

3. Do I know what a clear-Havana cigar is? No. It is in keeping with Salinger's general style of providing a bevy of minute details about a character that have no immediate bearing on the plot's forward motion but lend a certain reportorial tone, as though Salinger, via Buddy Glass, is saying: "I'll share all the facts with you and we'll have to do our best to make sense of it." Later on, when the "tiny elderly man smiles," providing a very uncomfortable Buddy with enormous solace, his smile is described: "It was a grin that was no less resplendent for the fact that it made no sense whatsoever. Nor for the fact that his teeth were obviously, beautifully, transcendently false."

small boy with a red balloon had run into the cleared, forbidden street. He had just been captured and was being dragged back to the curb by his father, who gave the boy two only partly open handed punches between the shoulder blades. The act was righteously booed by the crowd.

"Did you *see* what that man did to that *child*?" Mrs. Silsburn demanded of everyone in general. No one answered her.

What's particularly interesting about this passage, in the context of *Carpenters*, is that Buddy's rather intrusive voice disappears for a moment, and we are left with Salinger's clear, unfettered narrative of a scene, in that slowed down, real time about which I was talking. I love this passage, and yet, all this worship of a divine child, who is able to desire without complication, well, where does that leave you when you grow up (when desire always seems complicated)? Read: Where does that leave me?

I've been developing this nervous feeling that to live in the Salinger Weather means to harbor the opinion that grown-up life is corrupt and not worth living.

. . .

AT THE SAME TIME, I can get lost in rereading that scene, laughing out loud with delight in the same way I do when I read the part in *Catcher* where Holden riffs about how "I act quite young for my age sometimes." And then goes on to explain that the right side of his head "is full of millions of gray hairs." And finally: "Sometimes I act a lot older than I am—I really do—but people never notice it. People never notice anything." At such moments I'm reduced to the I LOVE JD SALINGER bumper-sticker mode.

But then a problem pops up, a familiar one, a problem many writers are likely to have encountered in one form or another when they read something they love. Yes, yes, it's very inspiring and all, but there is also the feeling (sometimes) where, upon reading a beloved passage you think is great, you think: "That's it. It's all been said, it's all been done, can't top that, forget it, I'll be a bike messenger or bartender or go to law school or something like that."

You see, there is part of me that wants to write an essay called "Killing Daddy: Overcoming the Anxiety of Influence." It would be about heroes. Hero worship, hero hatred, or, if hatred is too strong a word, then resentment. We need people to aspire to, and we need to outgrow our role models. At some point you have to kill Daddy. Or love him. Or both. All writers are, at least at one point in their lives, a little like Seymour Glass when he tells his readers in a diary entry: "I have scars on my hands from touching certain people." Well, just reading someone can scar you.[4] And then you ask: well, is it a good scar?

As I said, I began rereading Salinger when I had figured out that he was a reference for Anderson. I suppose my reading Salinger has been slightly colored by the enthusiasm of my friend's worldview, his style, though not too much. I mention

---

4. Just last night I read a three-page John O'Hara story and was like, "Holy shit! I want to do this, too!" I can't pick up *The New Yorker* more than once a month; even now, in its diluted form, the house style is too infectious. Who knows what strange corruptions a lifetime of daily *Times* intake has caused?

it at all to illustrate what I think is one of the most salient characteristics about Salinger as a writer: he is a master of tone. Is tone transferable? Can you imitate it, or imbibe it, or get scarred by it?

．　．　．

ONCE, DURING A nasty fight with an old girlfriend, I used this word—"tone"—in passing, and she exploded in invective at me at how superficial it was to place such a high premium on "tone" in writing. This outburst surprised me, because I hadn't thought I had made so much of it; it was one of those unnerving moments when it dawns on you that your repertoire of thoughts and observations is almost painfully finite, and that someone who has spent a lot of time with you has probably heard certain things a good many times, much like someone listening to a Top Forty radio station all day will hear the same songs in heavy rotation over and over.

In the midst of our fight I found myself stammering in defense of tone. Tone is that ineffable aspect of a piece of writing that is at once the hardest thing to actually define, and also its most central component. A book may be about a guy who is . . . I can't even finish the sentence, because the hypothetical possibilities are too numerous. The point I was trying to make, to stick closer to the subject, is that *Raise High the Roof Beam, Carpenters* is a story about a guy who goes to his brother's wedding, and then his brother doesn't show up. But that little synopsis has nothing to do with what makes it an affecting and memorable piece of writing. It's the diction, the syntax, the voice. Salinger is not a master of construction—he once remarked, "I'm a sprinter, not a miler"—but of something more elusive, the space contained within the structure.

Now, I admit that there is something almost willfully stupid about this opinion. If someone punches you in the face, the first thought is not, "What was the tone of that punch?" There is something loathsome, in fact, about such attention to tone, as it somehow sneers at the importance of actual events. And yet the writing that has most intrigued me has been winning because of its tone.

I was discussing the author Richard Yates with someone who was going on about how much he admired Yates. I concurred but then expressed the reservation that Yates's prose left me a little cold. "It's not the language, it's the penetration," was the reply. It was a good reply. Yates was able to get at deep human truths, and evoke real complexity in his characters, with a flat, affectless prose. I admired him for that. And yet I felt myself withhold from him my love. Maybe that was part of why that old girlfriend was so infuriated by my insistence on tone being such an essential detail in appreciation of a piece of writing—because it is ephemeral and elusive, and on some level, irrational. It doesn't make sense.

. . .

THE OTHER DAY I returned for a couple more pages—my quota it seems—of *Carpenters*. The early pages of that story are extreme Salinger Weather, almost suffocating. Our narrator, Buddy Glass, starts with an anecdote from the Glass Family Youth and then makes some commentary about the story he is about to tell:

It is, in my opinion, a self-contained account, with a beginning and an end, and a mortality,[5] all its own. Yet, because I'm in possession of the fact, I feel I must mention that the bridegroom is now, in 1955, no longer living. He committed suicide in 1948, while he was on vacation with his wife . . .

Seymour, subject of *Carpenters* and the emotional center of so much of the non-*Catcher* writing, is here, but not here. This is Salinger's great territory: he is the laureate of the here but not-here, of the presence of absence and the secret dialogues we have with those who are not in front of us to hear them.

The Salinger Weather is heavy with the romance of absence.

"I might add, not quite parenthetically, that he was by far the least prolific letter writer in the family," writes Buddy of Seymour early on in *Carpenters*. "I don't think I've had five letters from him in my life."

Since Seymour is generally presented as a kind of saint, a divine figure in possession of the deepest wisdom, it feels safe to say that Salinger is creating an equation between the non-prolific and the virtuous, the quiet and the good, between the people who think they have things to say and happily say it (i.e., the phonies), and the people who say little, but are in pos-

---

5. Fatality and Mankind are two words the thesaurus comes up with for mortality. The dictionary comes up with four definitions, three of which relate to death, and the fourth being; "The Quality of being mortal. Said of a sin."

session of some deeper wisdom, like Seymour Glass (or, perhaps, my friend Anderson).

As far as Salinger himself, I have no problem with Salinger up in the woods. None! I'm not interested in the daughter or ex-girlfriend's memoirs, I don't have any desire for the man to come down from the mount and start proclaiming.

But because I live in Salinger Weather, because I so enjoy the man's writing, because there are so many of the man's virtues that I aspire to in my own writing—the way he sets the scene, his faith in the importance of the small details of human interactions, his enthusiasm for using New York City as a stage set, the random nonsequitorial nature of the thoughts and conversations of his characters, his sense of the way people shift gears, the lostness and the vaguely comforting quality of this lostness that pervade his tone, his philosophical and essentially hopeful nature—I feel a little sensitive to how disappointed in the world he seems to have become.

In 1974, some "Berkeley Grad School types" had the enterprising idea of printing some of Salinger's uncollected stories in an unauthorized book that, unsurprisingly, "sold like hotcakes," according to one bookstore owner. When Salinger got wind of it he sued to stop them and was irate enough to agree to an interview with Lacey Fosburgh,[6] a reporter for the *New York Times*. He said

---

6. If you were to try and come up with a parody of a Salinger name, you probably couldn't do better than "Lacey Fosburgh." Of course maybe it's just because it's a WASPy sounding name, and, in spite of the Jewish/Catholic provenance of the Glass family there is something about Salinger that lends itself very well to WASP fantasies. Just the other day I came across an ad for Kate Spade bags—an accessory positively brimming with fifties nostalgia without any kitschy irony attached—that featured a woman reading *Raise High the Roof Beam, Carpenters*. To all this I reply: not Salinger's fault. Though I wonder if J. D. belongs to a sub-phylum of WASP-loving Jewish writers, and I'm not talking about the Rothian shiksa-goddess. It's a love that transmutes itself, in which the writer himself becomes, somehow, an emblematic Brooks Brothers man.

he'd speak for "only a minute" and then went on for half an hour. He said: "Some stories, my property, have been stolen. Someone's appropriated them. It's an illicit act. It's unfair. Suppose you had a coat you liked and somebody went into your closet and stole it."

Well, let me interject here, since I can't pretend to be just riffing on a writer I love—as coeditor of this book, I have helped perpetrate a whole ensemble of writerly musings—that neither me nor anyone else wants to steal his coat.

. . .

ACCORDING TO THAT same *Times* article from November 3, 1974, Salinger also said: "There is a marvelous peace in not publishing. It's peaceful. Still. Publishing is a terrible invasion of my privacy. I like to write. I love to write. But I write just for myself and my own pleasure."

That sounds so healthy and well-adjusted and cool, unless you happen to be a writer, in which case there is an odd hint, a suggestion, that to write with any hope of having other people read it—to be loved and paid for your writing—is corrupt. So if you really admire Salinger, does that mean you have to stop publishing? Of course not. But the question lingers.

. . .

THE OTHER DAY, a friend of mine said of Salinger, "He's really very punk rock."

"Why is that?" I said.

"Because he is against the system. He's anti. He's anti-literary establishment. He's anti–every kind of establishment. He's just anti."

Is Salinger anti-development? Is he anti-growing up?

"Development" is a pretty multifaceted word whose definition, according to *Webster's Third New International Dictionary*, is:

> 1: The act, process or result of developing: the state of being developed: a gradual unfolding by which something (as a plan or method, an image upon a photographic plate, a living body) is developed: gradual advance or growth through progressive changes: Evolution.
> 2 a: the whole process of growth and differentiation by which the potentialities of a zygote, spore, or embryo are realized; *broadly.*

Well, you can't just race past a word like "zygote," which the dictionary defines as: "a cell formed by the union of two gametes."

A gamete, I went on to discover, is: "a mature germ cell (as a sperm or egg) possessing a haploid chromosome set and capable of initiating formation of a new individual by fusion with another gamete."

The definition was prefaced with several examples of the word's Greek roots, all of which pertain to marriage in some way, and which conclude with the following directive: "more at BIGAMY."

At any rate, it would be negligent to have come this far and not look up the pretty excellent-sounding "haploid."

The definition: "Having the gametic number of chromosomes or half the number characteristic of the somatic cells."

This would seem a sufficiently dry definition to kill the "Let's look it up!" game, but it is only the first of two. The second definition is: "a haploid individual," which I find rather beautifully circular and nonsensical; it's as if you looked up "googooblah" and the definition was, "a googooblah individual."

Even better, there exists the following word: "haploidy."

I can't say exactly why the word "haploidy" makes me happy—maybe because it seems like a combination of happy and hapless, with a *tiny* little suggestion of android—but it does, and furthermore, it puts me directly back in the Salinger scrutinizing camp.

What all this says to me is that the world is divided into the haploidians and gametians. The former are basically single and the latter are, if not married, then willing and able to couple (perhaps repeatedly; "more at BIGAMY").

And I would like to suggest that the little deaf mute uncle, who sits grinning and oblivious throughout the whole of *Carpenters*, is a Haploid. He is a kind of sublime Haploid. He is a world unto himself, a self-sustainer, someone whose spirits remain unharmed by whatever is going on around him because he doesn't really know or understand what is going on around him. Or maybe he understands it perfectly and is therefore able to be "delighted." Phonies are, invariably, loudmouths. The uncle's silence, then, seems like a virtue. He is certainly the only person in the cab who seems to be completely enjoying himself. He is a Haploid, and just about everybody else in the car—the furious brassy matron of honor, her surly lieutenant husband, the prim Mrs. Silsburn—is a Gametian, except, perhaps for Buddy Glass. Salinger's personal sympathies are with the Haploids. Seymour, for example, is more of a Haploid than a Gametian. Then there's Holden Caulfield who, in all of his loneliness and sorting through phoniness, is a shining beacon of haploidness.

The individual is so powerfully felt in Salinger's writing. It makes you fear for the unit of two (or at least the unit of two in which both parties are alive).

You see, there is the fear I have that if you're a Salinger fan, if you're living in the Salinger Weather, you can never have a relationship with another person. I mean a developed, adult, love-type relationship. Some people refer to this as marriage but I'm not a marriage fetishist and I mean it in the broadest terms: Salinger's heroes don't grow up. Reading Salinger, one gets the feeling that love and joy are so transient that to dip one little toe of adult reality into the clear pool of authentic emotions is, almost by the very act, to sully and destroy it.

Adult knowledge, in its most basic form, means sex. Now, the scene with the hooker in *The Catcher in the Rye* is great— and I have forever wondered what, exactly, the hand gesture was that the pimp performs on Holden's crotch that hurt so much—but aside from that, it is notable how little outright leering and lusting and plain old horniness there is in Salinger's general oeuvre.

Not that it is entirely absent: Seymour Glass looking at Sybil's foot in "A Perfect Day for Bananafish" becomes less innocent when seen in the light of his suicide half an hour or so later.

Even more than Holden, Seymour embodies the most vexing and antagonizing aspects of the Salinger philosophy, the feeling one gets while reading him that Love is the most exalted condition, so exalted no mere mortal can perform it, or that those who really can, such as Seymour, can't survive in our world.

With Seymour, and, come to think of it, with my friend Anderson, the important details are communicated almost through something like clairvoyance, a kind of spiritual, non-verbal energy, transmitted by certain objects, that emanates from certain people. Maybe as I get older I've developed a resistance to this, the old boring tendency of grownups to resist the magical. Because that is at the heart of Salinger's appeal: he makes things so human, but not mundane; or rather he makes the mundane wonderful, and so the magic trick is that in the Salinger Weather life seems incredibly worth living.

Who knows when I imbibed the Salinger Weather? At some point it got in there and it's been in me ever since. But I worry about it. Just because you love something at one point in your life doesn't mean you will love it with the same intensity forever . . . I meant that about writing, but it has a sort of chilling and antiromantic ring to it all around. Right away I want to protest and say, "No! No! Love is forever!" But I guess what I'm trying to say is that maybe it's time for me to let go of some old T-shirts.

An Unexamined Life

BENJAMIN ANASTAS

"The human voice conspires to
desecrate everything on earth."

—SEYMOUR GLASS,
from Raise High the Roof Beam, Carpenters

I.

Of all the private documents that have lately found their way
into print under the abused publishing category known as
"memoir," only one, Margaret A. Salinger's *Dream Catcher*, is
so unequivocally removed from the realm of literature—so
inward-looking, so ungenerous, so artless—that it achieves a
perfect state of irrelevance, the nadir, if you will, of the autobiographical practice, revealing falsehood where it seeks to ex-
pose the "truth," and truth where it reveals the hollows of the
secret-teller's damaged little heart. The secrets broadcast here
are weirdly fascinating in their own right: childhood sex abuse;

unexplained psychic "sensitivities"; a possible UFO abduction at summer camp; multiple personality disorder; alcohol abuse; bulimia; chronic fatigue syndrome; abortion; and numerous miscarriages. (Among the less severe "traumas" cataloged are food poisoning, altitude sickness, and receiving "unlovely" presents for Christmas.) Most fascinating of all, however, are the glimpses we are offered of Margaret Salinger's absent father, the silent bard of Cornish, New Hampshire, and—in a strange twist of fate—the ultimate progenitor of *Dream Catcher*:

> My father once told a friend that for him the act of writing was inseparable from the quest for enlightenment, that he intended devoting his life to one great work, and that work would be his life . . . for such *maya* as living persons to get in the way of his work, to interrupt the holy quest, is to commit sacrilege. I was nearly middle-aged before I broke the silence, broke the family idol guarding generations of moldy secrets, both real and imagined, and began to shed some light and fresh air, wholesome and life-giving as Cornish breezes.

That the same wind that had buffeted J.D. Salinger's secret life since 1965 (the date of his last voluntary publication) should inspire his daughter to air her gripes out in public is an irony that will cheer the therapists of love-starved children everywhere. This reader is reminded of Nabokov's rejection of the "vulgar, shabby, fundamentally medieval world of Freud" and his "bitter little embryos spying, from their natural nooks, upon the love life of their parents." Privacy, more than ever, is a virtue from a world before the talking cure, and in one fell swoop—or two, counting Joyce Maynard's *At Home in the World*—J.D.'s flight into the woods becomes a farce complete with flannel nighties, homeopathy, Mary Jane sneakers, Dianetics, girls' basketball, urine-drinking, crying fits, and an orgone box. A vow of silence is broken by the literary equivalent of a clock-radio alarm; a mystery devolves into finger-pointing; the reclusive author's idyll is ransacked by the whirling devil of our age: honesty in black-and-white.

II.

I had never realized that I might also be a child of J.D. Salinger until, in the months before my first novel, *An Underachiever's Diary*, was published, two separate writers from different ends of the cultural and political spectrum, in providing quotes for the jacket, made comparisons to Salinger's work. One accused my narrator of being in league with Holden Caulfield; the other heard an echo of Seymour Glass in the novel's mournful-comic voice. I myself hadn't read a word of Salinger since my senior year of high school, having sloughed off this early influence (or so I thought) along with Ernest Hemingway, the New Wave fanzine *The Trouser Press*, and any and all records on the 4AD label. So I took these benefactors at their word and turned back to Salinger for clues, knowing full well that just about any novel about alienated young adults invites comparison to *The Catcher in the Rye*.

And what a perfectly imagined world I found, especially in the twin bills *Franny and Zooey* and *Raise High the Roof*

Beam, Carpenters and *Seymour—An Introduction.* The Glass family, in all its ragged glory, seemed to me so different from the white bread subjects of "domestic" fiction written in Salinger's wake, so principled and articulate, so distinguished from the split-level ranch home, monosyllabic rabble that had come to dominate American short fiction in the 1980s and early 1990s.

Perhaps it was my innate sense of urbanism, having grown up in the melting pot of Cambridge, Massachusetts (Boston's Upper West Side), or the fact that, like most readers of "*A Perfect Day for Bananafish,*" I first came to the story at an impressionable age and was, on some level, still reeling from Seymour Glass's suicide (how encouraging, then, to read of a Glass family still suffering from his absence, to devour Buddy's multiple attempts to wrest some meaning from his brother's life). No matter what the underlying cause, it seemed I had forgotten—if, indeed, I had ever known—that Salinger meant the world to me; and as a reader first, and as a writer second, all my apparent sophistication melted away as I was fed straight from Buddy's hand (or so it seemed) that Seymour was "our blue-striped unicorn, our double-lensed burning glass, our consultant genius, or portable conscience, our supercargo, and our one full poet, and, inevitably, I think . . . our rather notorious 'mystic' and 'unbalanced type.' " Like Franny near the end of *Zooey,* padding down the hallway in her tie-silk dressing gown and growing "younger with each step," this reader was astonished, upon reading Salinger again, to find himself transformed into an awestruck child.

A due sense of proportion would return, of course, and I was reminded of why Salinger finds his ideal audience in young

BENJAMIN ANASTAS

adults, who are forgiving, rather than the fully formed, who are not: his reliance on dorm-room theology; his Balthusian reverence for little girls (confirmed, sadly, by the Maynard and Salinger memoirs, which record the human fallout); his sometimes jarring use of popular forms to communicate an antipopulist message. But I was also reminded, and too vividly for comfort, of a certain misfit at a prep school outside of Boston circa 1982—a scholarship student with a strange, unpresentable family and an "ethnic" last name that precluded his attendance at certain social gatherings—who, like countless young misfits before him and countless since, found in Salinger an ally against a world-at-large that seemed unspeakably corrupt.

This unhappy soul had been raised by liberals of the sincere, eternally outnumbered variety (picture a Danish fondue pot, a Siamese cat named Sappho, and a record collection that stopped growing with George Harrison's *Concert for Bangladesh*), and suddenly found himself, after taking the PSAT exam on a lark, surrounded by three hundred junior Captains of Industry in Brooks Brothers jackets and nautical-themed ties. At prep school he was not ridiculed so much as ignored—an even worse fate in a society where exceptionalism was the rule—and while he learned, as all outsiders must, to accept the judgment of his peers ("Hey, who's that faggot over there?"), he could never accept the way the members of the faculty, knowing nothing of his makeup, looked him up and down and seemed to disapprove. *Is it the haircut*, he used to wonder, *or the single earring? Do they know my jacket is secondhand? Is there something terrible about my shoes?*

His days on that sprawling campus were spent in a search

for friendship, and when he eventually found it—and even, over a course of many months, began to make a place for himself among the lunkheads and the high achievers—he began to experiment in the fine art of teenage cruelty. "Burn in hell!" he used to yell across the chapel lawn. (*The boy shows little respect for the sanctity of tradition*, the faculty pronounced.) At an absurd break between periods known as "cookies and milk," he became especially adept at picking off squirrels and even the odd chipmunk with his "ration" of brittle, industrial food products. (*When around his peers, the boy tends to "act out" in order to receive attention*.) The school's newspaper, under his editorship, published a fake "Miller Lite" ad featuring two alcoholic members of the faculty. (*The boy has once again disappointed us with a clearly inappropriate use of "humor."*) But he did have one unadulterated joy on that campus—a favorite class, taught by his favorite teacher: "The Hero as Rebel-Victim," an elective in English presided over by Mr. John Muir (called "Jack" by his colleagues but never by his students), an elderly Southerner with a fondness for Harris-tweed jackets and the novelist Walker Percy.

Now, it's important to note here that most of the boy's classes were needlessly boring, and most of his teachers were, as the saying goes, an open book. Mr. Muir, on the other hand, cultivated a genial, sphinx-like quality, and, as a consequence, the rumors swirled. One had him married to a Southern belle forty years his junior; another claimed that he had been, in his prime, a nationally ranked tennis player; yet another had him commanding an all-black Marine battalion during World War II. For his part, our misfit imagined that a search of Mr. Muir's home would reveal, in a bottom drawer of a rarely used hardwood desk, the manuscript of an autobiographical novel typed on onion-skin paper—indeed, there were times in Mr. Muir's classroom when he thought that he could smell the thing.

Need I say that it was in Mr. Muir's classroom where he first communed with J.D. Salinger? Or that, when he felt the urge to write himself and scrawled out his first short story on a yellow legal pad, he took a calculated risk and gave the manuscript to Mr. Muir for his comments?

Mr. Muir was not the kind of young, energetic teacher who sought to involve himself in every aspect of his students' lives. He did not give more than he had to, which is to say, he taught his classes well and truly, but when they were over, they were over—life went on. Our misfit had caught him checking his watch while the "A" students monopolized another discussion period; he had waited patiently with the rest of the students while Mr. Muir, spotting a potential tennis partner through the windows, called the man inside his classroom to set a court time. And most curiously of all (our misfit could never quite figure out if this ritual was an inspired idea, the product of convenience, or both), once a month, always on a Friday, Mr. Muir would spend the last half hour of his classes reading aloud folk tales in Gullah, the language spoken by former slaves and their descendants on the coastal islands of Georgia and South Carolina. Even our misfit was aware, at his early age, that there was something potentially fishy about a white Southerner reading the folk tales of slaves—in dialect—to a 99-percent white student body. (He was also aware that the few black students who walked among them were no more "real" to his classmates than the original speakers of Gullah.) But he also sensed, on those Friday afternoons, that something remarkable might

be happening; certainly the English language had never resonated with quite the same expert force, carrying far and wide,
it seemed, across the campus to the world beyond. It would not
be until he read Joyce (another wake-up call) that he would
hear again, in literature, what he thought to be the sound of a
beating heart, transposed to the page by a hunted, haunted
writer.

This was the teacher with whom our misfit chose to share
his inaugural attempt at writing fiction, an homage to the
Museum of Natural History scene in *The Catcher in the Rye*.
Mr. Muir seemed surprised to receive this gift from a quiet,
just-above-average student, but he accepted the manuscript
gracefully. A few weeks passed. The misfit managed to concern
himself with other things (meaning girls from their sister school
in Boston). Finally, at the end of a class period just before the
semester's close, Mr. Muir called his name for perhaps the first
and only time, motioned for him to approach his desk, and removed his manuscript from a worn leather briefcase. His classmates were filing out with the usual groans and chuckles, and
barely took notice of the drama. "Here's your story," Mr. Muir
said, handing the pages, which had begun to curl, back to his
hapless pupil. "I don't know what it means," he went on, "but
I hope you'll keep on writing." That was it! No comments on
the failures of style or content; no exegesis of the story's awkward use of symbolism; no checks or exclamation points in the
margins (he would sit down in a hallway of the science building
later on and check the manuscript for pencil marks). Was he
upset? Strangely, no. Discouraged? Hardly—he would return
to his dorm room that very night and begin work on another
short story. This narrator would like to gently suggest that our

misfit, for the first time, had come into contact with Kao, the clever judge of horses from Seymour Glass's favorite Taoist tale—the only judge who can spot the "superlative horse," an animal that "raises no dust and leaves no tracks," "evanescent and fleeting, elusive as thin air." What misfit, in his heart of hearts, does not believe that he is a "superlative horse"? And would not long—in a world full of lesser judges—to be judged by Kao, who in "making sure of the essential . . . forgets the homely details"? ("So clever a judge of horses is Kao," goes the story, "that he has it in him to judge something better than horses.") Many years later, our misfit would find his own small way of thanking Mr. Muir for keeping his ineptitude their secret, but for now we'll leave him in the classroom, taking back his fragile yellow manuscript and feeling, despite the coolness of his teacher's tone, as if he'd somehow been anointed.

III.

Judging by the substance of her memoir *Dream Catcher*, Margaret Salinger and I have exactly one thing in common: both of our fathers are writers. Mine has not written books that are widely read or taught universally in schools, nor has he inspired pilgrims and paparazzi to visit him at his Cape Ann hideaway. He is a writer by every other scale of measurement; that is to say, he has given his life to the solitary pursuit of making narrative, some of which has been published, and some not. (Seymour Glass's two questions for Buddy come to mind: Were most of your stars out? Were you busy writing your heart out?) My parents divorced when I was three for reasons that are now evident, and I was raised, for the most part, under the shelter of roofbeams supported by my mother and her "partner."

Still, every other weekend when we were growing up (that is, my older brother, twin sister, and me), my father drove to Cambridge in his blue VW Bug, picked us up at our mother's apartment, and brought us north to the town where he was born—the kind of time-sharing arrangement familiar to many children of our generation. We spent the weekend doing the usual things that families do—going to museums; visiting our grandparents; eating meals together and talking about our lives—but for some reason I remember Sundays best of all, the day we were due to go back "home." Sunday mornings started early with cartoons, a heart-thumping hour of professional wrestling, followed by a ritual breakfast of eggs and bagels around ten o'clock. After the various showers and a romp around the yard (weather permitting) came a sandwich, and then commenced another Sunday ritual, our biweekly waiting game: our father waiting to be delivered from the demands of parenthood; my brother, sister, and me waiting to be returned to our independent lives, which took place back in Cambridge (friends, schoolwork, and especially for me, video games at Elsie's in Harvard Square). We were captives, both parties, pinned in that living room by ritual and blood—yet the bond that kept us seemed strangely tenuous, dependent, as it was, on the days of the calendar and the hour on the clock. Now that I'm a reasonably happy and productive adult, I've come to blame the sadness that sometimes visits me on Sunday afternoons, especially in winter, on those childhood Sundays when biology was not enough.

And I'll always remember, too, how my father, an inveterate journal-writer, took his black ring-binder out from its hiding place and sat at the kitchen table during the final stages of our waiting game, beginning to write about our weekend (or whatever else was on his mind) before the weekend was over, laying claim to our shared experience by writerly prerogative. I sometimes wonder if, had my father's audience been dramatically larger than it was (he sometimes wrote about us in his newspaper column and in pieces for upstart literary journals), I would have felt more cheated on those Sunday afternoons—one of three children sitting at his feet, yet to leave the house and already passing, as he wrote quietly away, into the realm of personal mythology. Does this explain my failure to keep a journal of my own? Or my reverence for the imagination and its ability to change the personal, to transform experience into something else?

It's a paradox, of course, that the pursuit of literature—which depends so squarely on life—should require its agents to live at a certain distance from what they choose to venerate by writing; but in a perfect world, where everybody loved each other all the time and with perfect sensitivity, there would be no need for narrative—or any other form of artifice, for that matter. (Life would be enough.) Writers walk a fine line, doing what we do, seeking always to strike a balance between polar opposites: what to reveal, and what not to reveal; when to eavesdrop, and when to grant life its rightful sovereignty; whether to write for one's self alone, or whether to write for an audience (i.e., to publish); indeed, whether to write at all, or whether to remain, like the felled tree in the empty wood, silent. (A retreat best described by Buddy Glass in one of his parenthetical asides to the reader, "Oh, you out there—with your enviable golden silence.")

Pity the writer's child for discovering, early on, that parents don't always want their children underfoot, that love is not always returned in the way that it was given, that fictions are sometimes more prevalent than truth, even in the "safe haven" of the family. But don't pity the discovery itself, not for a minute—for what the child loses in illusions, he or she gains in the capacity to feel gratitude for what life offers in reality. One would have thought that Margaret Salinger, of all the writers' children in the world, would have a better grasp on the numberless value of what remains unspoken; that she would have found a way, somehow, to avoid indulging in the kind of confessional writing that her father, in a more comic vein, once described as taking on "precisely the informality of underwear." As it is, the secrets are out, the dirty laundry has been aired, and nothing is changed, really, but for another dream of "wellness" written, bound, and cast atop the discounted pile in the memoir section. And at what cost? Another dream, just as foolish, coveted by Seymour Glass and shared by kindred spirits everywhere—the peace, the quiet, the respite, the *relief* of an unexamined life.

Holden Schmolden

AIMEE BENDER

There was a selection of doodles I drew repeatedly during English class in high school. The most popular item was a large eye. It had long lashes and a lid and a finely combed brow and a carefully shaded iris. Also well-represented was the cube, which I'd draw in 3-D, by utilizing that handy trick of making one box, and then another box, and then adding the diagonal lines between the boxes. Eye, cube, eye, cube. As a variation, occasionally I'd make a cube on a post, which I found inexplicably satisfying. Never an eye on a post. Sometimes an eye on a girl, but noses were hard, as were lips, so usually the singular eye just looked steadily off the page, and never spoke or heard a thing.

I did not like to pay attention in English class. Books scared me.

At the start of my sophomore year, I'd filed into Mrs.

Stevens's room, sixteen years old, nervous. My brand-new denim notebook had dividers with cellophane labels that opened to each subject. English always claimed the first slot, bright and chipper under yellow plastic. English was my strong suit. I dreaded English class.

Mrs. Stevens was only about five feet tall, but her reputation was big. She'd make you write papers thirty pages long, about at least two books. She'd wiggle around the classroom in her owl-round glasses and shriek mighty statements about literature. If she liked what you wrote, you'd get an A+++++++++++ and you and your friends would compare; Samantha got three plusses; Matt got seven. An actual A+ would be a letdown.

Stevens started each year with *The Lord of the Flies*, and every morning, right after the bell, a different student would blow loudly into a conch shell swept off some Santa Monica beach. That set her off. She tore around the classroom yelling, "Piggies! You're all Piggies!" I had no idea what she was talking about but I made a little dot at the corner of my eye doodle to indicate a tear duct. Stevens stomped in front of her blackboard, brandished a pointed stick in the air, and yelled: "They sodomized the sow, bubies! They sodomized the sow!"

She called us all bubies, all the time. I tried not to sit in front. Get away, weird lady.

I had no idea how to write an essay. I was terrified of actually putting a thought onto a page. I couldn't stand to explore mystery or complexity because at the time the entire world of adolescence seemed overwhelmingly mysterious and complex, and concrete things, i.e. synonyms, were far more appealing. So I pored, with earnest intent, over the long list Stevens passed out: One Hundred Ways to Say "Moreover"—*likewise, in addition*; One Hundred Ways to Say "Show"—*promulgates, exemplifies, elucidates, illustrates.* For the ideal Stevens essay, you were supposed to write a synonym for moreover, then state the author's name, then use a synonym for show: *In addition, Golding elucidates . . .*

I was so grateful for her five-paragraph essay equation because to make writing like algebra seemed to me, at the time, perfect. Stevens wanted us to simplify the complicated. To explain and back up and unpuzzle. To boil down. She wanted us to make a point, and usually she told us the point to make. I studied books for grades alone, and had lost my appetite for reading.

The Catcher in the Rye did not reinstate it. That took a much longer time. Nothing could slip through the block I had built against books; the words themselves felt like they were written out of barbed wire. Don't come in. I was having a lot of trouble making the transition from the magical adventures I'd read and loved as a child—journeys through closets and tunnels—to novels about Serious Topics. I did not understand war according to Stendhal, I couldn't quite relate to Fitzgerald's take on New England society, I didn't comprehend Maugham and his book on Gauguin whose paintings I'd only seen on postcards, and I was not even interested in reading about sadistic island children. I was interested in any kind of book with raised print on the cover that you could drop into the bathtub by accident, and rediscover, the next morning, as a bloated wet gray wavy mass near the drain.

But I do remember when Stevens reached into a cardboard box and pulled out tiny copies of that burgundy cover with orange print. Our next book. That book. I turned to the front flap and signed my name after last year's book owner—George Woo—a senior of no particular distinction. If you were really lucky, you got a book that someone cool from last year had used. That was true currency in our high school world.

Once all signed and accounted for, Stevens scanned across her students, beady-eyed.

"You," she announced, pointing to the blondest, most handsome boy in the room.

"Me?"

"*You* will be our Holden while we discuss this book."

This was Southern California, and no one here looked remotely like a prep-school kid; my high school was ten blocks from the beach and full of surfers. Pink-skinned peeling boys who woke up at five in the morning to curl up in the ocean before class started at eight. Their hair whitened by salt. I imagined prep-school boys to be pasty, not tan; to wear button-up shirts, not shorts, in December; I imagined Holden himself to be shadowlike and angular, not robust and sun-bleached. For my class, Stevens picked a boy named John Carlson, who my friends and I referred to sometimes as J.C., i.e. Jesus Christ, i.e. our savior babe of all time. We were mostly a dark-haired, dark-eyed Jewish clan, and these surfer types were the most verboten of beauties.

John Carlson's job was easy. He just sat there. Sometimes she referred to him with a wave of her teacherly hand, or she asked his opinion and he laughed, uncertain, and she said, "See, Holden? See, Class?"

"Bubies! He's right here among us!"

So he was, smelling of the ocean, and I was blissfully off

the hook. Anonymous. I was a girl after all, and I was perfecting my very detailed iris and pupil and next to my bed were wavy soggy pulp books and who goes to prep school anyway.

We moved through the year, we took SATs, we graduated, we wrote tear-stained yearbook elegies, we disappeared.

Truth was, J.C. wasn't so far off the mark as a Holden rep. He, even with his bright white smile, seemed slightly outside the mainstream of our high school world. When asked, surfer-types tended to talk with reverence about how calming it was to contend with the ocean every morning, and didn't have much patience for anything else. Surfers hated phonies as much as anybody. So what happened, then, to these assigned Marine Holden types? What's the future of a Southern California Holden?

I decided to e-mail some high school friends, to see if they had any idea what might've happened to any of Stevens's picks. Who were the other chosen Holdens? I was curious; perhaps a former Holden might be drawn to a certain job type. Perhaps I could create a Holden theory of growing up: Holden as world traveler! Holden as organic chicken farmer! Holden as high school teacher! I eagerly awaited the e-mail replies, hoping those who'd been listening could fill me in about a time when I'd been up to my elbows in rows of perfect cubes.

But when I heard back from everyone, the response was unanimous.

"We don't remember either," they said. "We don't remember Stevens picking out anyone at all. She did what?"

I wrote to others.

"I remember those essays that took forever," said one. Another had an update on John Carlson. "He's lawyer with a new baby," she said. "He's doing fine. He was assigned to be what?" No other names came forward. The entire Holden selection had slipped from their minds. Did I invent the whole thing in my memory? Was that how I related to the book, by turning my high school crush into the lead character? Or, if it was real, then how many eye doodles were going on in that class, staring up at the ceiling with mine? Truth was, in this wildly informal poll, no one I e-mailed really even seemed to remember discussing *The Catcher in the Rye*. Everyone recalled the big papers and the outrageous grades. We remembered our grand adjective-packed theses about alienation. But the books?

It took me until after college before I really remembered why I loved to read in the first place. I had plain and cleanly forgotten. I was starting, finally, to challenge this idea I had ingested that all famous books were by nature dull and stodgy, and I was discovering that there were tons of writers who were much weirder than I ever knew, and rejoicing like crazy at this discovery. It was like rediscovering breathing. One of these writers was Salinger. I was living in San Francisco at the time, and my friend Miranda was reading him and rereading him and she gave me *Nine Stories* as a birthday present because I was trying to write some short stories. I was in a very conservative short story mode, thinking overly about craft. I'd crafted myself into a small wooden decorative box at a flea market, five dollars and ninety-five cents.

Nine Stories is an anti-craft. Just look at the title, for God's sake. And it was *Nine Stories* that wooed me most fully with its wonderfully free emotional narratives and oddly surreal gestures. Reading it made me realize that even though he had been discovered ad nauseum by the world, one of the magical feelings about reading J.D. Salinger was that you, yourself, felt like you were discovering this writer for the first time and had made him yours in the discovery. Salinger invites possessiveness, in the best way.

So many of the stories I'd been reading in writing classes and anthologies reminded me of circles—they felt unified, whole, realistic. But Salinger's moved in squiggles or lines— he'd start in one place and end abruptly somewhere else, and there was no pretense, no crap. Take it or leave it. These were odd stories and they were intimate. And as well crafted as they were, they didn't obey any rules about what makes a short story "work," and reading them helped me regain an innate trust in the inexplicable pull of natural storytelling. This is such a rare feeling. With few exceptions, I didn't feel this kind of absolute freedom from a whole collection again until recently when I finally picked up *Jesus' Son* by Denis Johnson, and bam! That same wonderful hard-to-describe combination of relief, and envy, and wonder, and *permission*.

I went back then, and read the whole Salinger collection— those books with their great seventies shades of oranges and burgundies on the cover—and they all blew fresh air into the bookshelf. Even though it took him nine years or something to write, it feels like Salinger wrote *The Catcher in the Rye* in a day, and that incredible feeling of ease inspires writing. Inspires the pursuit of voice. Not his voice. My voice. Your voice. Give that eye doodle a mouth, finally. Speak.

I remember reading *Nine Stories* in my little San Francisco bedroom, which had a view of Sutro Tower and various over-grown backyards, and thinking, with a great and tender tendril of hope: This gets to be literature? This? This is not barbed wire. This is not even fancy. Look at how he ends "The Laughing Man"—so sudden and so done. In the middle, the boy has a tangerine in his pocket and there's no reason for it except there's a tangerine in his pocket. I don't know why these stories stick in my mind but they do, and I can't solve or undo them or copy them or boil them down or figure them out.

Talk to me about mystery now: I am ready.

I like to think that somewhere out there exists a massive troop of grown Holdens. Stevens's team. She's taught at my high school for probably over thirty years now, so here we are, from ages nineteen to forty-nine. Throngs of us, doodlers and all. Some Holdens must have teenagers of their own by now, reading the same book, with the same burgundy cover and orange print. Discovering—or not discovering—that wash of sadness and joy.

In one of my favorite stories, "De Daumier-Smith's Blue Period," Salinger's narrator is a young man who is writing a letter to a nun in correspondence art school. He's intent on telling her about the happiest day of his life, reentering the world for lunch with his mother after she'd been sick, when "suddenly, as I was coming in to the Avenue Victor Hugo, which is a street in Paris, I bumped into a chap without any nose. I ask you to please consider that factor, in fact I beg you. It is quite pregnant with meaning."

Oh, so unexpected! So right, and inexplicable! Moreover, likewise, furthermore. Promulgates, exemplifies, illustrates.

In addition, Salinger elucidates . . .

. . .

WITH GREAT GRATITUDE, I am still considering it.

The Yips

JOEL STEIN

There is a terrible pleasure in not writing. Think back to college, right before a paper was due. Everything was more exciting: sex, sleeping, football, *Melrose Place*, even talking. For a writer, every nonworking moment is like that. I have built my investment portfolio, called my grandmother back, even got in there and cleaned the individual electric razor blades with the short end of the brush the day an article was due. The closer to deadline I am, the more productive I become at nonwriting activities. Once, just three hours before I had to hand something in, using nothing more than a diagram in a magazine, I taught myself how to tie a bowtie.

But some writers are so powerful and so rich, so deadline-proof, they are able to extend the procrastination—even indefinitely. Joseph Mitchell, the second most famous nonwriter of last century, still went to his *New Yorker* office in a suit and tie every day until he died in 1996; he hadn't written an article since 1964. And it wasn't because he was always getting shot down at pitch meetings. The first most famous nonwriter of the last forty years, J.D. Salinger, has not published since 1963. It's not like the guy retired to Thailand to do drugs and sleep with whores; that we could understand. He lives in New Hampshire. Not writing, it turns out, has the texture of hard, New England work.

Since finishing his first novel, *The Catcher in the Rye*, in 1951, Salinger has not published another one. There has never been a writer with a more influential first novel, especially among young people and mentally ill assassins. So is it the fear of a sophomore slump that has kept Salinger from writing? Discomfort with so much attention? A lack of confidence that paradoxically came from feeling overcelebrated and hence overrated? Or are there more hookers and coke in New Hampshire than we think?

In Gus Van Sant's movie *Finding Forrester*, the Salingeresque character, played by Sean Connery, says he hasn't written because his work is misinterpreted by scholars. Then, after a bunch of touching scenes, he says it has something to do with guilt about his brother's death. Then he's cured by baseball. It's not that good of a movie.

In *Field of Dreams*, baseball is again given salvific powers for the Salinger character. Salinger was, in fact, a baseball fan who dreamed of being the Yankees' center fielder. But perhaps baseball, more than offering a way out, demonstrates a parallel to Salinger's career. Every so often a player, usually a pitcher, will get the yips—suddenly be unable to perform. It's happened to Rick Ankiel last season, Chuck Knoblauch for the last few years, Mark Wohlers a few years before that, Steve Blass in the seventies; and in the fifties, Salinger's time, to Von McDaniel.

In April of 1958, Von McDaniel, one of the very few baseball players to skip the minor leagues and go straight from high school to the majors, was still only eighteen, and was coming off a terrific rookie season with the Cardinals: he shut out the Dodgers in his first game, later pitched nineteen consecutive scoreless innings, and even pulled off a one-hitter. He was sensitive, shy, intelligent—kind of like Holden Caulfield with a mean fastball. But at the beginning of his second season, McDaniel got the yips. He was sent down to the minors, where he was still dysfunctional, home plate eluding him all the way to Class D league; he wound up a farmer, and later an accountant, and finally a preacher before he died. He told a reporter that "maybe things came too easily."

I was hired as a writer for *Time* magazine when I was twenty-five years old. I had been writing on a weekly basis for a small, startup local magazine for two years before that. My first pagelong assignment at *Time* had me at a hotel in Minneapolis, sitting in front of my laptop from 10 P.M. to midnight, without writing one sentence. By 1 A.M., my screen was still blank, having erased every sentence after typing it. I visualized four million copies of my article; I saw kids not yet born viewing it on microfiche; I saw it being read by astronauts on the space shuttle, mostly because I was overtired and hallucinating by that point. I even pulled up to a White Castle drive-through right outside of Minneapolis, and when the woman asked me what I wanted, I said, "Just to talk." Eventually, the fear of losing my office with a TV in it overwhelmed my fear of failure, and I banged out the article on the video-game champion I had interviewed. It sucked, with forced, jarring sentences slapping against the backstop, but it got me by until the next week; and eventually, after a few weeks, I realized that the White Castle woman was right and that no one uses microfiche anymore.

Virginia Woolf, who was a Victorian aristocrat as much as a modernist, said one needed her own room, five hundred pounds a year (in 1928 money), a good meal, and a backrub in order to write. As a guy with a TV in his office, I can't really argue with that. But it's also possible that if you get too much recognition, if everyone else thinks you're a bigger deal than you do, you can be Barton Finked into losing the confidence necessary to write. Writing, after all, is based on the cocky belief that a mass of people want to sit still and listen to you talk for an extended period of time. It's pretty easy to get the yips.

Particularly when you've got to follow up on *The Catcher in the Rye*. I don't reread books or watch movies more than once, but I read *The Catcher in the Rye* every year. It's still the only book that's not sold in a porn shop that I've read in one day. And before my English degree forced me to claim that *The Sound and the Fury* or *Ulysses* was my favorite novel, depending on who I wanted to impress, *Catcher* was—and, when I'm not fronting, still is—the best book I've read. It tells more in the first paragraph than most novels ever do, and it has immortalized fifties slang. I can't get through ten sentences without throwing in a Caulfieldesque "and all" or "or something." Especially when I'm getting paid by the word and all.

I was twelve when I read *The Catcher in the Rye* for the first time, and I remember being shocked that a piece of literature could have the word *fuck* in it. That you could curse in a novel and not have it considered trash. That you could write like people talk. It taught me how honesty is reached through artifice—that the second person, extraneous conversation-alisms, and even hiding behind a character's voice, can get you closer to what you want to say. And knowing that those tools were available has helped me avoid the yips. That and the fact that I don't have enough money saved up to afford missing a deadline. Two years after I first read the book, we had to read it in school, and we were given the assignment to write a short story in Holden's voice. I nailed it. And the truth is, I never quite unlearned it.

A year and a half into my job at *Time*, the managing editor offered to give me my own column. My career goals had always been pretty clear: I wrote a column in high school, in college, and at *Time Out New York*, the magazine I worked at before *Time*. I figured one day I'd write a column for a local paper. I did not figure that local paper would be *Time* magazine. I did not figure I would get to do it at twenty-seven. At twenty-seven, I stopped being hungry. Every straight news story, every celebrity profile, every TV review I have written since has suffered from my fullness. People are always asking me what is next in my career—screenplays? novels? TV commentary?—and I tell them I am done. I don't want anything else, and while it gives me freedom and peace, it's also a little death, though without any of the advantages the French claim. Without the hunger, the need for an ego-fix, there's less to keep me writing.

So I'm starting to feel a little of what may have stopped Salinger from writing. It's a combination of being satisfied, being afraid to try something different, and hating the phonies who try to tempt you into writing point-of-purchase books that will make them money. When Holden says he is thinking about getting away from all the phonies, he suggests to Sally Hayes that they run away. "What we could do is, tomorrow morning, we could drive up to Massachusetts and New Hampshire, and all round there, see. It's beautiful up there. It really is," he tells her. When that doesn't pan out, he plans a hermitage, figuring he'll pose as a blind mute for the rest of his life.

I've been thinking about what Salinger is doing since I was fourteen. And I've convinced myself, for these fifteen years, that he's compiling a whopper of a novel, which no one will see until he dies. It will be a giant mess of a manuscript that every editor in New York will fight to get their hands on, and over the decades multiple editions will be released. It will be called *The Glass Family*. And it will make me cry.

I have been compiling facts to convince myself of this, that he doesn't really have the yips. Salinger, despite what everyone thinks, is not some freak hermit. He's married, goes to the supermarket, and as we learned from Joyce Maynard's book, likes to watch sitcoms. He also apparently likes to hit on very young girls. To be honest, I'm not sure what freak hermits do that is so different from this, but it's important for me to believe that they're not married sitcom watchers.

He also writes, though my proof here is a bit moldy. In a 1974 interview with the *New York Times* he said, "I like to write. I love to write. But I write just for myself and my own pleasure." Maynard says he writes but nobody is allowed to see the work. I use that excuse all the time with my editors.

Salinger has long been a Zen Buddhist. Part of Zen is to do something for the sake of itself; to chop wood not to have firewood, but just to get into a state of wood chopping. At least that's what I got out of my college course on Zen Buddhism. Still, it follows that one could write simply for the sake of creating, or for the meditative state you get when you're really writing in the zone—the way hours disappear and you don't hear the album you've played seven times in a row because you never heard it. To write without needing to have a one-sided conversation with the world—to write for the process and not the result, to be Emily Dickinson by choice, to pitch ninety-five-mile-an-hour fastballs into a net in your backyard—could be a higher level of writing. Maybe you can cure a case of the yips by shutting out the distractions.

In *Seymour—An Introduction*, Salinger writes, "Yet a real artist, I've noticed, will survive anything. (Even praise, I happily suspect"). Sometimes, he just needs to get away to do it. Why New Hampshire I'll never know.

Holden Caulfield: A Love Story

JANE MENDELSOHN

The winter I was eleven, we were still living in New York City. I say still because my mother and I were moving to Canada the next year to live in a city called Toronto, which sounded about as far away from New York, where I had lived my entire life and where my father would continue to live, as any place I could possibly imagine. It was a sad winter for me, especially over Christmas vacation, when there wasn't much distraction. I probably watched a lot of TV, but I had already watched so much TV in the first eleven years of my life that I was approaching the human limit. It might have snowed, I have a vague memory of a blizzard, but that would only have made the city more beautiful and me more sad. My sadness itself was mildly interesting—I told my friends that I was leaving next year as if I were going off to a sanitarium—but I couldn't devote an entire Christmas vacation to it. (I was only eleven.) So I read, probably with the television on, a lot of books.

I read whatever I could find in the apartment: *A Member of the Wedding*, *Dr. Spock's Baby and Child Care*, Agatha Christies, and it was somewhere in there, that winter while it was maybe snowing outside, that I first met Holden Caulfield. Saw the hat, heard the voice. Stood with him at one end of the corridor at Pencey while he called out *"Sleep tight, ya morons!"* with tears in his eyes. Turns out, I never went to boarding school and never ran away from anywhere, didn't stay in a hotel by myself until I was out of college, and never walked to the lagoon in Central Park at night, but I never stopped looking for Holden Caulfield. I looked on the steps of the Museum of Natural History, by the bandstand in the park, in taxis. Where I really searched for him was among the boys I knew; I was always finding the lost ones, the ones I could squint at through some haze of coffee steam and sarcasm until they became the guy in the red hunting hat. Somewhere in the back of my mind, where it's always maybe snowing and the television's on low, I still believe that any day now I'll be running away with Holden.

I say all this because I'm probably not the only one. For me and I would guess a lot of other people, Holden Caulfield set the tone for a certain kind of long-lasting literary crush. It seemed impossible that I could ever fall out of love, that I could ever outgrow Holden. His voice provided an inner soundtrack that played in the background of my every romantic misadventure. It's a scratchy, funny, knowing and know-nothing riff that makes you dream each new frog will turn into a prince but lets you know, with a cutting remark that sends you back on yourself, that you have, in fact, just kissed a toad. In Holden's world, no one ever has to fall out of love because romantic love is always unrequited or impossible.

Rereading the book as an adult, I realized that all of the objects of Holden's affection were unavailable. Who are they? Jane Gallagher, the girl of his memories now going to football games with someone else (it didn't hurt my own crush that her name was Jane); his dead brother, Allie; his little sister, Phoebe, who loves him but is too young to understand his teenage angst (she loses patience with him for not liking anything); and the Museum of Natural History ("I loved that damn museum"). In Holden's world, love is wrapped up like a mummy. His failing history essay is about the Egyptians, what they used "when they wrapped up mummies so that their faces would not rot," and his visit to the Metropolitan Museum culminates in his showing two little kids the way to the mummies. I don't want to make too much of the fact that Holden seems really to be looking for his own Mummy, or Mommy, who has been very distracted, or perhaps even dead to him since Allie died, but then again why not? I think this is at the heart of the book.

In Holden's world, you can't go back to childhood—that's locked up in the Museum of Natural History, where Holden doesn't make it past the front steps—but you can't grow up either because growing up means becoming a phony. You can't really fall in love because real love with a real person might be less than perfect (this is the adolescent's dilemma), but you can't really do anything but look for love. It's a world in which if you really want to know the truth you can just get on a train and ride out west to a ranch. Of course, when you get there, the ranch might turn out to be Hollywood, or a psychiatric hospital. So maybe it's better just to keep looking for romance, not truth—to keep falling in love forever.

. . .

SO HOW DID IT HAPPEN? When did I start to fall out of love with Holden? It began, maybe, with the rumors about Salinger, old J.D., as Holden might call him, the tales that were later solidified in books that I couldn't bear to read. There was the affair with the Yale freshman when he was so much older; the orgone box; the drinking his own urine. If you really want to know the truth, I just didn't want to hear about it. What does it matter, anyway? Who cares about writers? It's the work that counts, right? But still, something seeped in, some stale smell of reality, or worse, depravity, that had always hung around Holden but that was more like a sharp cologne breezing off his preppy shoulders in the book, while in real life it just stank.

Maybe it was those stories that led me to pick up *The Catcher in the Rye* again a few years ago, when I was writing a screenplay about a teenage girl. Maybe this was the beginning of the end. Right away, I thought I'd found what I remembered: that voice, cocky and insecure, reckless and afraid, filled with jaded longing and innocent wisdom. There, on the second page, were two lines that summed up everything I had been feeling as I struggled to get my thoughts across in screenplay form: "If there's one thing I hate, it's the movies. Don't even mention them to me." At a time when I was working out my own feelings about the relationship between film and fiction, I found Holden's protestations funny and touching. All that ambivalence, the love-hate that gives the book its happy-sad tone, its aura of playful melancholy, I felt it conjured so much more than adolescence, but also American life, the stupid beautiful movie of it all. (Of course, Holden is actually obsessed with the movies—witness his death scene at the hotel—but he sees through the myths. This is what spoke to me while I was trying to reconcile what I loved about movies—the gorgeous surfaces, the layering of sound and image, the dreamlike power of enacting events—with what I loved about books: the interiority, the ability to radically, and inexpensively, compress and expand time, the feeling of traveling through consciousness, the intimacy. I never did figure out how to get my ideas across in screenplay form, and eventually I ended up turning my script into a book. But that's another story.) Hey, I thought, this is great. Here I am, back with the snow and the TV on, everything comfy and witty and poignant and familiar.

So imagine my surprise as I began to read further, and, with the so-called wiser perspective of adulthood, I discovered that *The Catcher in the Rye* isn't really a book about a smart-funny-preppy New York teenager running around town by himself for a few days and looking for romance or at least understanding, but that it was a book about a *suicidal* smart-funny-preppy New York teenager. It was *all about death*.

. . .

MY REVELATION CAME SLOWLY. I just started noticing all the references to death, and many specifically to suicide. It's pretty innocuous at first. There's the "It killed me" on page two about D.B. being in Hollywood, and then, at the bottom of the page, the talk about the football game: ". . . you were supposed to commit suicide or something if old Pencey didn't win." On page four Holden tells us that he "got the ax," and by page five that "you felt like you were disappearing." Still only on page five, Mrs. Spencer asks Holden, "Are you frozen to death?" and the next thing you know he's being ushered into Spencer's room, where the old man appears to be lying, practically, on his death bed.

I didn't make too much of this, but then the references really started pilling up, like, say, dead bodies. On page nine, Holden talks about his gray hair; on page eleven, about the mummies; on fourteen, about a remark Spencer makes, "It made me sound dead, or something." On page seventeen, "That killed me" reintroduces the recurring phrase that I eventually counted at least thirty-five times, and by page twenty, "You were a goner." On page twenty-two, Holden says of his hunting hat: "This is a people shooting hat . . . I shoot people in this hat." And so on, and so on.

I couldn't believe what I was reading. I'd remembered that Allie's death figured in the book, that some of Holden's mental state was a response to his loss, but I hadn't realized the magnitude of it, the scale and depth and burden of his despair. For the first time it occurred to me perhaps why Holden's hunting hat is red: because Allie had red hair. And I saw new meaning behind Holden's comment that "I act like I'm thirteen." Although he's sixteen when the book takes place, he was thirteen when Allie died. I'd never understood Holden's urgent desire to know where the ducks went in the winter when the pond froze, but now I got it; he wanted to know where Allie had gone, and where he could find his mourning and unavailable mother.

Holden's mother. Mrs. Caulfield. There's somebody I'd thought about for maybe one second. I'm not even sure I could have told you whether she appeared in the book. Turns out she does, in the scene where Holden returns home and talks to Phoebe. Actually, right before Holden comes home, he imagines his own funeral and feels especially sorry for his mother because "she still isn't over my brother Allie yet." In the middle of his conversation with Phoebe, (during which Phoebe says several times that "Daddy'll kill you" when he finds out that Holden's been expelled again), their parents come home. Holden hides in the closet and his mother questions Phoebe about the cigarette smell in the room; "Now tell me the truth," she says. I could hear her saying that a million times, to the point where naturally Holden would begin his confessions with the line "If you really want to know the truth." He's talking, in a sense, to his mother.

Of course the kind of truth Holden's mother is asking for isn't Holden's brand of truth. He cares about emotional truth, and perhaps this is what resonates so strongly for kids when they first encounter the book, the recognition that there's a difference between the two kinds of truth and that negotiating between them marks the beginning of the end of childhood. The first half of the novel reads like a descent into the truth at the center of Holden's solitude. His journey from school to the hotel to hiding from his mother to the lonely encounter with the prostitute culminates in the punch from Maurice and Holden's acting out a death scene from the movies: "I sort of started pretending I had a bullet in my guts," he says. He pictures himself staggering around, plugging Maurice, and having Jane come over and bandage him while holding a cigarette for him to smoke. It's a sendup of everything phony that Holden hates, but a revealing display of his true feelings at the same time. In his gunfight fantasy, he's *concealing* the fact that he's been shot; in reality, he's been trying to hide his despair. At the end of his B-movie reverie, whether or not we want to know it, he finally tells us the truth: "What I really felt like, though," he says, "was committing suicide."

Holden's admission marks the halfway point of the book. He spends the second half trying to find someone to talk to about his feelings, someone who really wants to know the truth. He tries the chilly Sally, the condescending Luce, the gentle, intelligent Phoebe, who responds with all her love but who's too young and innocent to see that he's desperate, and finally, his ex-teacher Mr. Antolini, who lectures Holden and then proceeds to make a pass at him. And why does Holden seek out Mr. Antolini? Because he was the one who finally picked up that

> boy that jumped out the window I told you about, James Castle. Old Mr. Antolini felt his pulse and all, and then he took off his coat and put it over James Castle and carried him all the way to the infirmary. He didn't even give a damn if his coat got all bloody.

So there it was: the boy of my dreams wasn't so funny after all. He was miserable. That killed me.

. . .

I MENTION ALL of this death stuff not as a way of saying that there should have been more teen hotlines in the 1940s, but to describe how completely different the experience of reading

The Catcher in the Rye was for me after so many years. It was like running into an old boyfriend and realizing that not only has he lost all his hair or gained fifty pounds, but that he was *always* bald or overweight or depressed or hostile or just plain crazy, although you had no idea at the time. It was, frankly, a little unnerving, but humbling as well. I didn't actually love *The Catcher in the Rye* any less; I just wasn't in love with Holden anymore.

And I appreciated the book in a new way. In understanding its darkness, I could see it as more than a *beautifully effective* or *fully imagined* coming-of-age story, but as a work of almost gothic imagination. As Leslie Fiedler says, all of American literature is fundamentally gothic. In the end I found references to death on almost every other page, and this relentless awareness of death and the language of death, of common phrases that embody darker meanings, this language obsessively alert to itself, seems to me the sign of something closer to art than not. Thoreau said that "Writing may be either a record of a deed or a deed. It is nobler when it is a deed." I do think that *The Catcher in the Rye* is a noble book. Messed up, but noble.

So what about Holden? I'm not in love with him anymore, but do I still love him? Last week, I took my eighteen-month-old daughter to the Museum of Natural History for the first time. We saw the canoe, the whale, the dioramas. She ran around pointing at everything and squealing and the guards were all incredibly nice and the lights were soothingly dim and everything smelled musty just like I remembered and, with the exception of a few exhibits, it seemed as though nothing had changed since I'd been there as a kid, and probably since Holden had walked the halls.

Toward the end of our visit my daughter got tired and stretched out her arms and said, "Up." I picked her up and held her for a little while and then we got ready to go, and as we strolled out onto Central Park West and I felt the huge gray museum sleeping solidly behind us, I thought about Holden. I thought about his name, about how he just wanted to be held. And I thought about how physical books are, how you can hold them in your hands. When you're young and you read a book, it seems to hold you, creating a world around you, but then as you get older, you can hold onto it; your own world takes on a life of its own, bigger than any book but able to contain many worlds, many stories within it. Maybe that's what makes a book great, if you can grow up with it, never outgrow it exactly, but find a way to pick it up over the years and form a new connection.

As I pushed my daughter's stroller into the park, she started to fall asleep, and the image of the museum began to melt into the trees. But before it disappeared completely, I thought I could see Holden, the boy in the hat, the one I first fell in love with, and the boy all alone, the one I just wanted to put my arms around. I thought I could see him, waiting for me on the steps.

Contributors' Notes

Benjamin Anastas is author of the novels *An Underachiever's Diary* (Dial Press, 1998) and *The Faithful Narrative of a Pastor's Disappearance* (Farrar, Straus & Giroux, 2001). Other writing has appeared in *GQ*, *Story* magazine, *Tin House*, *The New York Observer*, *The Village Voice*, and the online magazine *Salon*.

Thomas Beller is the author of two works of fiction (*Seduction Theory*, stories; *The Sleep-Over Artist*, a novel) and is a founding editor of *Open City Magazine* and mrbellersneighborhood. com. His work has appeared in *Best American Short Stories* and *The New Yorker*, and he is a contributing editor to *The Cambodia Daily*.

Aimee Bender is the author of a collection of short stories, *The Girl in the Flammable Skirt*; and a novel, *An Invisible Sign of*

My Own. Her short fiction has been published in *Granta, GQ, Harper's, Paris Review*, and more.

Karen E. Bender is the author of the novel *Like Normal People* (Houghton Mifflin, 2000). Her fiction has also appeared in magazines including *The New Yorker, Granta, Zoetrope*, and *Story*, and included in the *Best American Short Stories* and *Pushcart Prize* anthologies, as well as the series *Selected Shorts*. She lives in New York City with her husband and son.

Charles D'Ambrosio lives in Seattle. He is a graduate of Oberlin College.

Emma Forrest's first novel, *Namedropper*, was published in 2000 by Scribner. A Londoner, she left school at sixteen for a career in journalism. She has had columns in *The Times* of London and *The Guardian* and contributes regularly to the *London Telegraph*. She has also written for *Vogue, Vanity Fair, The Face*, and *Marie Claire*, and has just completed her new novel, *Thin Skin*. Now twenty-four, she lives in New York City.

Aleksandar Hemon is the author of *The Question of Bruno* (Nan A. Talese, 2000). He was born in Sarajevo in 1964. He now lives in Chicago with his wife, Lisa Stodder, a Chicago native.

Walter Kirn's latest novel is *Up in the Air*, published by Doubleday. He is the literary editor of *GQ* and a contributing writer at *Time*. He was educated at Taylors Falls Public High School, Princeton University, and Oxford University. He lives with his family on a farm near Livingston, Montana.

John McNally is the author of *Troublemakers*, winner of the John Simmons Short Fiction Award in 2000. He's the editor of two anthologies. *The Student Body: Short Stories About College Students and Professors* and *High Infidelity: Great Short Stories About Adultery*. He's won several awards for his fiction, including a James Michener fellowship, a Wisconsin Institute for Creative Writing fellowship, and a scholarship from the Bread Loaf Writers' Conference. He is currently the Jenny McKean Moore fellow at George Washington University in D.C.

Jane Mendelsohn is the author of two novels, *I Was Amelia Earhart* and *Innocence*. She lives in New York City with her husband and daughter. Her essays and reviews have appeared in the *New York Times*, the *New York Times Book Review*, the *London Review of Books*, *The Guardian*, *The Village Voice*, *The New Republic*, and *The Yale Review*.

Lucinda Rosenfeld's first novel, *What She Saw . . .* , was published by Random House in 2000. She has written essays and criticism for the *New York Times Magazine*, *Harper's Bazaar*, *Elle*, *Talk*, *Word*, *Slate*, *British Vogue*, and *Beauty the Rite Way*, the free circular distributed by Rite Aid pharmacy. Her fiction has appeared in *The New Yorker*. *What She Saw . . .* may or may not be a major motion picture in two years, starring any number of dewy-skinned ingenues. She lives in Brooklyn, like a lot of other people she knows.

Amy Sohn is the author of the novel *Run Catch Kiss*. She was born in 1973 and is a graduate of Brown University. She lives in Brooklyn and is writing a new novel, *Are You My Daddy?*

Joel Stein is a staff writer at *Time*, where he writes entertainment, sports, and a little bit of news and technology. He has written seven cover stories for *Time*. He also does a weekly column for the magazine. He used to work at *Time Out New York* during their first two years. Now twenty-nine, he went to Stanford (undergrad, and they gave him a master's in English). He grew up in Edison, New Jersey, and he loves his parents.

René Steinke is the author of the novel *The Fires* (William Morrow, 1999). She is an associate professor of English at Fairleigh Dickinson University and senior editor of *The Literary Review*. She is currently at work on another novel, *Holy Skirts*.

Acknowledgments

The editors wish to thank:

Their families.

Their teachers, especially:
Lawrence P. Colan
Aaron Hess
Barbara Kosty
Samuel Pierson
Paul Russell
and
William Gifford

And special thanks to Becky Cole, without
whose effort this book would not exist.

Bibliography

Bergson, Henri Louis. *Laughter: An Essay on the Meaning of the Comic.* Los Angeles: Green Integer, 1998.

Bonhoeffer, Dietrich. *Letter and Papers from Prison.* New York: Simon & Schuster, 1997.

Cronin, Gloria L., and Ben Siegel, eds. *Conversations with Saul Bellow.* Jackson: University Press of Mississippi, 1994.

Didion, Joan. "Finally (Fashionably) Spurious." In *Salinger: A Critical and Personal Portrait,* edited by Grunwald, Henry Anatole. New York: Pocket Books, Inc. 1962, pp. 84–86.

Freud, Sigmund. *General Psychological Theory.* New York: Simon & Schuster, 1998.

Hamilton, Ian. *In Search of J. D. Salinger.* New York: Vintage Books, 1989.

Kazin, Alfred. "Everybody's Favorite." In *Salinger: A Critical and Personal Portrait,* edited by Grunwald, Henry Anatole. New York: Pocket Books, Inc., 1962, pp. 47–57.

Leenaars, Antoon A., ed. *Suicidology: Essays in Honor of Edwin S. Shneidman*. Leonia: Jason Aronson Publishers, 1993.

McCarthy, Mary. "J. D. Salinger's Closed Circuit." *Harper's Magazine*, October 1962.

Maltsberger, John T., ed. *Essential Papers on Suicide*. New York: New York Univerisity Press, 1996

Maynard, Joyce. *At Home in the World*. New York: Picador USA, 1998.

Salinger, J. D. *The Catcher in the Rye*. New York: Signet Books, 1953.

———. *Franny and Zooey*. Boston: Little, Brown Books, 1961.

———. *Nine Stories*. Boston: Little, Brown Books, 1953.

———. *Raise High the Roof Beam, Carpenters* and *Seymour: An Introduction*. Boston: Little, Brown Books, 1963.

Salinger, Margaret. *Dream Catcher*. New York: Washington Square Press, 2000.

Schneidman, Edqin S. *The Suicidal Mind*. Oxford: Oxford University Press, 1996.